# Forgiveness: Key to the Creative Life

*Its Power and Its Practice—Lessons from Brain Studies, Scripture, and Experience.*

## Rev. James G. Emerson Jr.

Bloomington, IN  Milton Keynes, UK

 authorHOUSE®

*AuthorHouse™*
*1663 Liberty Drive, Suite 200*
*Bloomington, IN 47403*
*www.authorhouse.com*
*Phone: 1-800-839-8640*

*First published by AuthorHouse 12/5/2007*

*ISBN: 978-1-4343-0801-6 (sc)*
*ISBN: 978-1-4343-0800-9 (hc)*

*Library of Congress Control Number: 2007902799*

*Printed in the United States of America*
*Bloomington, Indiana*

*This book is printed on acid-free paper.*

*Photograph by Stephen Phillips*

# Forgiveness:
# Key to the Creative Life

*Lessons from brain studies,*

*Scripture,*

*And experience*

*By James G. Emerson, Jr. PhD*

*Preface by James A. Donahue, PhD, President of the*

*Graduate Theological Union,*

*Berkeley, California.*

# Three Communities of Faith and a Woman of Faith

*To members of the Brain Studies Task Force of the Society for Pastoral Theology* who prepare caregivers–clergy and lay--across the country. Without their encouragement and guidance, I would never have presented this effort for publication.

*To the people of Calvary Presbyterian Church, San Francisco* whose enthusiasm at lectures on this subject encouraged me to present this material for people of faith to read. Many told me that neurological studies had contributed to the creativity of forgiveness in their own lives.

*To physicist Carl York and others of the Center for Theology and the Natural Sciences at the Graduate Theological Union (the GTU) in Berkeley where Kelley Bulkeley and Mark Graves* lecture and write in the field of brain studies and allowed me to share in their studies and work; and to *Stuart Plummer and his late wife Maxine,* whose leadership in clinical pastoral education continues as a model in the field of care.

The GTU understanding of field theory, of neuroscience, and of the "Divine" provided the intellectual context in which the ideas of these pages could develop.  Stuart and Maxine's interest in attachment theory gave focus to me throughout the study.

*To Margaret*:  Ours has been a marvelous experience of "life together." In her years as a wife, mother, counselor, and friend she brings to us all the gift of healing, wholeness, and creativity.

# Table of Contents

# Preface

The test of quality for a work of scholarly creativity is always whether it rings true to the experience of the reader. In *Forgiveness: Key to the Creative Life*, James Emerson is able to strike a chord that will resonate deeply not only with scholars but with practitioners and lay people alike. Emerson explores how recent research in cognitive studies correlates with insights and ideas of religion and theological studies and the other humanistic disciplines, to create greater understanding about the process of human healing.

This book is an extraordinary example of interdisciplinary research. Emerson's experience as a scholar of religion, as well as a pastor with extensive experience with individuals in their developmental process, gives him fluency with both the scientific and theological material that is at the heart of his study. He is able to illuminate what this material really means in the lives of individuals like you and me who are navigating the vicissitudes of their life's journey. Jim is a thinker who builds bridges, not just in ideas and concepts, but in language and illustrative example. This book is extremely well written, is accessible to the reader, and always makes the link between ideas and practice, between theory and the real world.

Emerson is an astute interpreter of cognitive theory and shows the link between the existing studies and the theological ideas and religious practices central to the experience of forgiveness. Forgiveness is a phenomenon that is intrinsic to the human condition and is present in all dimensions of experience. At the personal level, navigating conflicts requires forgiveness for resolution and growth is central to human life. At the level of institution, social group, and community, forgiveness is requisite for the successful realization of social harmony and meeting personal goals. In these pages, Jim Emerson serves as a seasoned guide through the varieties of language, intellectual constructs, and social paradigms that address issues of forgiveness.

Emerson's study is at its core not only interdisciplinary, but inter-religious, theoretically sound and practically helpful, creative, and inspiring as well. His ability to intertwine multiple modes of investigation and to use categories of analysis and language that bridge these different perspectives in an integrated study is a remarkable achievement. Emerson does us a service as well by bringing some of the historical theories and ideas that have been part of our intellectual traditions, but perhaps left out of the contemporary conversation on forgiveness, back into the discussion.

This work will stimulate the thinking of both scholars and practitioners who are involved with the role of forgiveness in human life, religious or otherwise. We will talk about Emerson's ideas and be grateful to him for stimulating us to think and for bringing disparate ideas into an integrated whole. We will enjoy reading this book.

James A. Donahue
February 23, 2007

# To the Reader
## Why this book?

Some fifty years ago, my interdisciplinary graduate studies at the University of Chicago took me into the role of forgiveness as a dynamic in personal and community health. Seven years ago, a book entitled *Forgiveness* came on the scene. This book edited by Professors McCullough, Pargament, and Thoresen, and published by the Guilford Press, called attention to my book of over forty-years entitled *The Dynamics of Forgiveness.* They identified it as probably "the first scientific inquiry into the association of forgiveness with mental health and well--being."

Between that time and now, we have had the "decade of the brain" (1990-2000). As I have studied the lessons of that decade and since, I have asked myself, "How would I have written that earlier book had people known then what we know now about the brain?"

This book is the result of that question.

The fact is that new information keeps coming so fast that any thoughts we have today may be corrected or seem obsolete tomorrow. Yet enough has happened that we can stop and ask the impact of brain studies on the functioning of the brain in the experience of forgiveness. For all of us, this effort is a work in progress – but it is a progress we should identify. Few have made that identification.

The use of such procedures as brain scans, PETs, and fMRIs (functional magnetic resonance imaging) have confirmed some facts about forgiveness as an experience and shed new light on the dynamic process itself. Clearly, forgiveness is a powerful tool for coming to terms with life. Forgiveness, properly understood and properly used, leads to healing and wholeness in the lives of individuals and of communities.

Periodicals of all kinds now write about the brain or forgiveness – *The Economist, Newsweek, The Wall Street Journal, Time,* to mention a few. Research centers such as those at Stanford, Vanderbilt and other universities around the country have produced excellent work.

Yet what interests me most at this point is the research of people like Catherine Bushnell of McGill University Medical Center in Montreal, Canada, and Tom Farrow of the Sheffield Medical Center in Sheffield, England. They have focused on either forgiveness as such (Farrow) or empathy (Bushnell) without which the *dynamic experience* of forgiveness is lost.

I am fortunate. Both people have shared their research. Tom Farrow has continued to share his efforts.

Every caregiver can benefit from understanding how forgiveness really works. The caregiver may be a professional or a lay member of the family who offers help to a family member. Unfortunately much of the current excitement has lost sight of work that has already been done. One would almost think that no one did anything from the days of Sigmund Freud and William James until 1990! Those of us who seek to help need access to the insights of the past and the present.

As a result, I have two goals: First, out of experience to identify what of the new information is helpful for the present; second, to say enough about the past that we not "reinvent the wheel."

Kelly Buckeley and Mark Graves at the Graduate Theological Union, Berkeley, and John Hogue of Garrett Theological Seminary in Evanston, and Leonard Rosenman M.D. of UCSF have helped me greatly with evaluation of current brain studies. In fact, their continuing encouragement has kept me at this project. My friend of long standing, Herb Anderson now of Pacific Lutheran Theological

Seminary, has proved a source of help in not losing sight of the contributions from our own field of special studies of psychology and faith. William McGarvey, Pastor of the Community Presbyterian Church in Pittsburgh, California, read the whole manuscript and made constructive observations and comments.

I must mention Pamela Cooper-White of Lutheran Theological Seminary in Mt. Airy, Philadelphia, and Stuart Plummer of Denver and Fraser, Colorado. Dr. Cooper-White gave needed insights into the matter of rape and forgiveness – some of which is reported in her early book, *The Cry of Tamar*. Stuart Plummer and his wife Maxine added much not only to the matter of attachment theory but to my own general thinking as this book began and progressed.

I come to all of this out of a background of work with people such as Carl Rogers, Seward Hiltner, and Sandra Brown from the recent and distant past. I should also mention my indebtedness to James Lapsely, formerly of Princeton Seminary, and the Society of Pastoral Theology over the years. They have listened to my developing thoughts.

My wife Margaret, better known as Migs, and I have been so closely involved in our teaching over the past fifteen years that I had hoped we would co-author this book. Unfortunately, that was not possible. Margaret has been a creative critic. Yet, as always in such cases, I must carry responsibility for what is written.

Basically, I am a practitioner who specializes in what is called "evaluative research." "Evaluative research" is a form of research in which the researcher is part of the experience being studied. As such, the researcher must account for his or her personal influence on the outcome of any study. I live in both worlds of practice and research

For the purposes of this book, I give few footnotes and even less of a bibliography. Instead, I give attachments and comments at the end that will refer the reader to several books that have wonderfully extensive bibliographies.

Here, for both those in the practice of any form of care, counseling, care-giving, and mental health, I offer four observations as a beginning point.

1) *Field theory* from physics, both as a reality and as a metaphor, can help our understanding the dynamic activity of the brain and of forgiveness. Field theory gives us a common ground for seeing science and religion as related, not opposites.

2) *Capacity for creativity* stands at the heart of the dynamic of forgiveness and must be part of any definition--at least for communities of faith that have roots in Abraham (Islamic, Judaic, and Christian traditions).

3) *The dynamic of harmony* as understood in Asian thought, and particularly Confucian cultures, must be seen as part of the experience of forgiveness–not just the guilt-innocence model of Roman law.

4) And, *forgiveness as an experience that leads to a doctrine* must be the starting point. Too often we seem to begin with a doctrine into which we try to force an experience. The drive for wholeness and wellness requires a dialogue between practice and doctrine.

# Why These Four?

Forgiveness serves as a dynamic foundation for personal and social health—and provides for that health in us as individuals *and* us as parts of a community.

Those communities may be our own internal fields of feeling, thinking, and acting or the wider fields of our families, our closest friends, our places of work or play, and our communities of faith. (Studies by Farrow and Bushnell demonstrate the point.)

Equally important, the dynamic of forgiveness frees us to deal *creatively* with insults, threats, and betrayal rather than just react. I have come to understand the role of "field theory" in a way I never did before. Field theory gives us a metaphor, and more than a metaphor, that helps in understanding brain functions.

Field theory also becomes the basis for a dialogue between faith and science. Faith and science then become partners, not enemies, in ones faith and practice.

My conviction about field theory grew out of recent studies done on Michael Faraday -- a nineteenth century physicist whose work became basic to such legendary figures as Planck and Einstein. I will say more about Faraday in the section on field theory. Here, I simply commend the recent biography by James Hamilton, *A Life of Discovery* (Random House, 2002) and the portrait he gives of Faraday.

As we will note later, Kurt Lewin's work of the days before and after World War II became famous for his application of field theory to social issues. That work demonstrates the fact that our communities are as much in need of the dynamic of forgiveness as any individual.

# A Word about the Writer

I am a reader of works on cognition and neuroscience. I am not a professional in either field. My practice of ministry and my roles as an administrator of social services use the insights of pastoral theology, social psychology, and neuroscience.

My studies were interdisciplinary. In fact, my parents were interdisciplinary as is my wife and as our grown children

Amongst them all we have lawyers, administrators, and social workers, who have background in education, business, and theology. Family experience ranges from work in the inner city to dealing with the damage done by hurricanes and tsunamis. Some of our family have built in "habitat for humanity," others have operated at the highest levels of government, and still others have done basic research that has received international interest.

## My Experience with this Dynamic Itself

My first efforts in the dynamic of forgiveness came when I studied the issue of divorced people who wanted to get on with their lives and, ultimately, marry again. This focus grew out of the failed marriage of my own parents.

Out of my work with the subject biblically, psychologically, and sociologically, I came to the conclusion that a person could marry again only after he or she had experienced forgiveness.[1] I coined the term of that experience, "Realized forgiveness." Perhaps that is why the dynamic experience of realized forgiveness has fascinated me the rest of my life and why my studies back then resulted in my definition of forgiveness as related to creativity.

Creativity is a power, and its use takes different forms. Around the world, some cultures do not have the word "forgiveness" in their language. I think particularly of some tribal groups in Africa and some areas of China. However, those cultures do speak of freedom – especially the freedom for creativity. Where the word "forgiveness" does not exist, we still find words and processes that describe the power of forgiveness that takes on increased meaning for social thought. That creative power is a tremendous resource. Based on both psychological evaluation of case studies and biblical study, that theme of creativity continues as central to human life whether or not a culture has the word "forgiveness."

## *This Book*

This book divides into three parts and an epilogue. I have added some material as attachments that I hope may be useful.

The first part reviews the basic organization of the brain and addresses specific fields within the brain – shame, memory, and empathy. This section ends with discussion of methods for evaluating case studies or events that come from the Bible and from human experience. The perspectival method of Jerome Feldman, a specialist in cognitive thought at the University of California, is important here. Equally significant for this book are the methods of correlation by the late Paul Tillich, a philosophical theologian of the last century, and Christof Koch of the California Institute of Technology in Pasadena, California.

The second section then discusses the process of forgiveness itself. After a look at the biblical contribution to understanding the process of forgiveness (Chapter IV), I move on in Chapter V to examine three events taken from the Bible and three from current life. Biblical "cases," if I may use that term, involve Job, Jesus, and a man Jesus healed. Case events include the assassination of John F. Kennedy, the Columbine school shootings, and the shootings in the Amish school. The section closes with a look at ways in which Christian communities of faith have tried to make forgiveness "real"

The last section on the practice of forgiveness divides into two chapters. Chapter VI looks at significant events in church history that focused on the realization of forgiveness in personal life. Chapter VII then looks at selected life situations – in business administration, in life under oppression, in pre-marriage counseling, in worship, and in a death. In the epilogue, I touch on the implications for future thinking in several areas such as architecture and the use of space. To have gone into those matters in the body of this book would have broken the flow of thought but need mention.

In all of this, two points need to be clear:

1) My focus is on the experience of forgiveness itself whether or not a person is forgiving another or is seeking forgiveness from another. I personally believe that one cannot forgive others without first being able to forgive oneself. I further believe that reconciliation, redemption, and similar matters of faith may result from forgiveness but are a different type of experience than forgiveness. This book centers on the experience itself.

2) The question arises as to whether or not everything is forgivable. I believe there is that which is unforgivable and will write of that briefly. How that spells out in practice, however, depends on every individual case and will not be the basic focus here.

With the prayer and good wishes for the power and the practice of forgiveness in your own lives, let us begin the journey of this discussion.

James G. (Jim) Emerson Jr.

San Francisco, 2007

# Part One

## Field Theory and the Brain

### Abstract

*Field theory in the physical sciences and the Holy Spirit in the biblical sciences become basic points for understanding the brain and the practice of forgiveness as a choice.*

Chapter I is not different from any description of the brain with one exception – that emphasis on field theory. I call attention to field theory as a metaphor that correlates with understanding the Holy as a dynamic process and not just a theological doctrine. What physicists speak of as a "field of force" and what students of the Bible speak of as the Holy Spirit serve as the background in this section and the Bible in the next section.

With the background of field theory and workings of the "spirit" we come to a view of what it means to speak of "self" or "person" or "who we are."

For one thing, many of us conclude that we as individuals are more than just biological organization. *We as persons are always in the process of becoming – of becoming anxious and becoming whole, of becoming individuals and becoming attached in relationships; of becoming sinful, failed, or ashamed and of becoming whole, creative and free.*

*We shall come to see forgiveness itself as a process.*

*Forgiveness is part of the process of becoming.*

In Chapter II we will consider three basic "fields" -- Shame, memory and empathy.

Chapter III looks at the method of correlation and the perspectival method as the basis for applying the scientific method to the study of interpersonal relations generally and the process of forgiveness specifically.

# Chapter One
## Our Brains and Ourselves

### *An Event of Identity*

At the old Peoria State Hospital in Illinois, a patient spoke with me after a service of worship. I asked this patient, "What is it that you look for when you come here to chapel?"

Without a moment's hesitation he said, "I come here because when I do, it helps me remember that I may be sick, but I am still me. With my confusions, fear of persecution, and everything else, I am still me--and it helps me remember that when I am here."

To get the feel of this chapter, take a moment to ask yourself what it means for you to be you. Who are you? Who are any of us as created individuals who can laugh, cry, move, think, feel, love, sleep, and act? Do we get angry? Do we blame? Do we forgive–or at least have the capacity to forgive? Do we love? Can we experience love?

I ask those questions as we try to get a sense of what it means to think of us as people with a brain that functions. I think of us as a people with minds and I go on to ask, "Are our brains and our minds the same?"

## *The Biological Self*

It may seem strange to begin by speaking of field theory in relation to the biological question, "What is the brain?" Yet my first instructor in biology did exactly that in high school

R. J. Jungerman, the biology teacher of Palo Alto High School in the 1940s took a sheet of typing paper and placed it over a rectangular magnet. The magnet had two poles–a north and south or positive and negative. Mr. Jungerman sprinkled iron shavings from the shop on top of the paper. The shavings fell in a pattern that fanned out from each end with something of a flare design. This flare was not the field. The field itself was an invisible force. The students saw only the effects of that field of force–but all knew the field was there.

Why in the world did R.J., the biology teacher, show us this experiment from the world of physics? Not until many years later did most of us recognize that he saw all truth as one. R. J. saw that truth in one area of study had implications for other areas of study. The first lesson of that experiment taught us the reality of qualitative differences. We can measure the strength of the force and describe it. Yet, the force itself we saw as *qualitatively different* from its effects.

## *More Than Computers*

The reality of that difference still gets debated. Several years later, college students at Stanford, heard another biologist, the late Prof. A. J. Carlson of the University of Chicago. He said to a student, "Young woman, the only difference between your brain and your kidneys is biological organization."

The noted philosopher Daniel C. Dennett of Tufts University writes with wit, insight, and clarity. His book *Consciousness Explained* is "must reading." In a most sophisticated way he comes to the same conclusion as Professor Carlson. Professor Dennett writes,

"Human consciousness is *itself* a huge complex of memes (or meme-effects in brains) that can best be understood as the operation of a '*von Neumannesque*' virtual machine implemented in the *parallel architecture* of a brain that was not designed by any such activities. The powers of this *virtual machine* vastly enhance the underlying powers of the organic hardware on which it turns, but at the same time many of its most curious features, and especially its limitations, can be explained as the by-products of the *kludges* that make possible this curious but effective reuse of an existing organ for novel purposes."[2] (The italics are by Professor Dennett.)

Prof. Dennett anticipated a puzzled reaction and unpacked the jargon in that paragraph as he wrote, "What is illusory or mistaken is only the view that I am some distinct substantial self who produces these connections [in the brain] in virtue of a totally non-behavioral form of understanding."[3]

In reading both statements, note the emphasis on a "meme" or body part and the emphasis on "parallel architecture." "Parallel architecture" refers to a computer and a type of computer connection. "Neumannesque" refers to one of the inventors of the computer. All these reduce everything to some dimension of the physical. As did Prof. Carlson, these statements say that the only difference between our brains and our kidneys is organization.

Carl Rogers, a psychologist noted for his work during the 1950s in Client Centered Therapy, and his colleagues took a similar view in their pioneering research: " ...this group has the conviction that Thorndike's dictum is essentially correct – that 'anything that exists, exists in some quantity that can be measured.'"

Yet many, including Rogers and his colleagues, recognized a qualitative dimension when they wrote, "Psychotherapy is, among other things, one of the most subtle arts known to man. It is a rich and delicate relationship in which the nuances may have more significance than the obvious elements."[4]

Two important contemporaries of Carl Rogers took those nuances to mean that there are qualitative differences. Gordon Allport, who headed the Harvard Department of Psychology and Gardner Murphy, who directed research at the Menninger Institute, wrote books on personality that took seriously the physical dimension. Yet, Allport, and Murphy never reduced the mind, or consciousness, or ourselves to just the physical organization. A thorough reading of Rogers indicates that neither did he.

Many of those who object to the concept of a person, or a self, or a soul, do so in reaction to the philosopher/mathematician Descartes. Descartes, famous for his statement, "I think, therefore I am," located the soul in the pituitary gland. He wrote of the "theater of the mind" that operated in our brains and allowed for a sense of self that "sees" things and operates on them.[5]

Descartes has become a favorite whipping boy of neuroscientists and philosophers today.

The failure of these criticisms is that they shoot down the explanation for a reality called "you" or "me" without looking at the basic issue raised by Descartes and others – namely the view that not everything that exists is physical. There may be qualitatively different realities. We can measure the effects of beauty on the brain, but we cannot measure beauty itself.

In this book, I hold that the life force is qualitatively different from the shavings or the pattern of the shavings shown on the white paper by R. J. Jungerman's demonstration.

As the hospital patient said, after all the measuring and all the diagnosing, "I am still me."

## *Needed: An Ounce of Humility*

The fact that we cannot see everything nor measure everything requires an attitude of humility. The mathematician turned philosopher, Alfred North Whitehead, wrote of standing before the truth and following it wherever it will lead.

A contemporary expert in brain research who exemplifies that humility is Dr. Michael A. Arbib, Director of the Brain Studies project of the University of Southern California.

Dr Arbib describes himself as a non-believer when it comes to the traditional sense of the soul. He recognizes that people have a religious longing and have a sense of soul. "Nonetheless" he writes, "I believe that all of this can be explained in terms of the physical properties of the brain."[6]

Dr. Arbib also wrote, "We cannot approach theology without some sense of the intricacy of the human brain."[7]

To me, the attitude behind that latter statement is a model of how to approach the subject of this book. Dr. Arbib and I would not agree on the matter of faith, but he demonstrates a sense of humility in the search for the truth. That humility allows him to become a constructive part of the discussion with those of a different perspective. Even as he allows one to see where he stands on the faith issue, so must each of us and so must I.

## *Meet Christof Koch*

As we go to the brain itself and the dynamic of forgiveness, I am encouraged by Dr. Christof Koch and his "neurobiological approach" to understanding the brain. Given that Professor Dennett came to a conclusion from Dr. Koch's writing opposite from mine, that encouragement may be surprising.

However, in his detailed and thorough book, *The Quest for Consciousness,* Dr. Koch writes that where there is no brain there is no mind.[8] From the standpoint of Jewish or Christian theology, that statement causes no problem. For both Jewish and Christian thought, the whole point of a concept of incarnation is that something qualitatively different from the body is known through the body. Jewish thought sees that incarnation in Hebrew history itself. Christian thought sees that incarnation in the person of Jesus himself. Greeks speak of the immortality of the soul rather than the resurrection of the body. Those Jewish thinkers who believe in the resurrection (and not all do) speak not of immortality but of the resurrection *of the body.* Christian thought does the same. There is no self without a body.

Therefore, what makes the brain different from any other organ of the body, such as the heart or the liver, is the fact that it sustains a mind.

For example, in the middle of the brain we find an almond-shaped organ called the "amygdala" and near it another organ called the "hippocampus." When these lose the ability to sustain immediate memory, a person has Alzheimer's. What makes the "amygdala" the "amygdale" and the "hippocampus" the "hippocampus"? Is it not the fact that their respective biological organizations incarnate and sustain memory – perhaps only short term memory, but memory nonetheless?

Dr. Koch concludes his book with a dialogue that makes the point:

"Interviewer: What about religion? Most people on the planet believe in some sort of immortal soul that lives on after the body has died. What do you say to them?

Christof: Well, many of these beliefs can't be reconciled with our current scientific world view. What is clear is that every conscious act or intention has some physical correlate. With the end of life, consciousness ceases, for without brain, there is no mind. Still, these irrevocable facts do not exclude some beliefs about the soul, resurrection and God."[9]

Precisely! Not all religious world-views square with science. In this book, I hold that what I write does square with science. Hopefully, what I write will deepen an understanding of faith, of how it works, and of how it works in relation to the dynamic of forgiveness.

For all these reasons, I believe that there is a self to forgive – a self that is qualitatively different from our neurological being but that is incarnate in our physical being and has what Dr. Koch calls "neuronal correlates of consciousness." In short, there is a self to forgive.

## What then is the Brain?

Traditionally, people describe the brain as a biological organ with three parts – the primitive or "reptilian" part, the mid-brain, and the cerebral cortex. The latter two are divided into hemispheres. (Pictures are so available in books and on the Internet that I will not go into detail here. Dr. Koch suggests the Internet location http://brainmap.wustl.edu. With a general search, I also have found amazing picture resources available. Here, I give a brief summary.)

## The Reptilian Brain

We should never consider the "primitive" part of the brain as of less quality or less importance than the other two parts.

This "primitive part" at the base of the brain and on top of the spinal chord houses those neurons and ganglia that allow all living beings to breath, have a heart beat, and respond to anger or danger. If any part of us is like a computer, the reptilian brain is. The book *Jaws* described the shark as something that simply responded to smell in the water, attacked or ate it, and went on in a way that is fine for the shark but not for the victim. Some say that there are no feelings in this area –only reactions. Sense danger; fight it or flee from it. "Fight or flight" is the motto.

We must not take this "primitive" area lightly. Without it, none of us would survive.

To get a sense of the difference between the reptilian parts and the rest of the brain, consider the experience of a Miss B.

Miss B fell unconscious. A virus had attacked this reptilian part of her brain. She almost died. After the virus died, she did not need to learn how to think again. She did need to learn acts of breathing, walking, talking, and doing all those things that are basic for life. For that reason, we will use the name "reptilian" rather that "primitive."

From the reptilian part of the brain, we move up to the next section that is generally called "the mid-brain."

## *The Mid-brain*

The mid-brain contains those areas basic for feeling, for seeing, for aspects of hearing, for many motor responses, for coordinating thought, coordinating action, and for the initial part of memory.

As one studies the brain "map" inside the front cover of Prof. Koch's book, the name mid-brain technically refers to an area just above the reptilian brain. In the popular use, however, the phrase "mid-brain" covers a number of brain organs that form an umbrella over the brain stem and push up against the cerebral cortex.

In this section of the brain, we find names such as the thalamus, the hypothalamus, the amygdala, the occipital lobe, the hippocampus, and the corpus callosum.

The corpus callosum has particular significance because it fosters communication between the left and right sides of the brain – the left and right hemispheres.

In many ways, the term "wired" seems to fit this region of the brain. For example, we can trace "wires" with regard to sight as does Dr. Koch in his mapping on that first cover page at the front of his book.

As we look at the chart and his commentary we read, "Optical information flows from the retina in a quasi-hierarchical manner through a large number of cortical areas."

We need to pay attention to that statement.

At the outset, it warns us not to put the brain or the mind into too neat a set of definitions or boxes. Note: the "wire" goes from the mid-brain "through a number of cortical areas." How easy it is to think of the cortical area as "thinking" areas and the other areas as only "functional."

On the contrary, the intermixing is subtle, real, and awesome.

Further we need to note the use of the word "reciprocal." "Reciprocal" means not only that what we see goes through the eye, hits the back of the brain, gets sent up to other areas for integration, and results in vision itself. Rather we have a two-way street. What we see through the organizing work of the forward part of the cortex, in some forms, may move back and influence what the eye itself takes in and then sends on to the rest of the brain for processing.

This phenomenon means that when we see, we influence what we see as much as what we see influences us! If that sounds tricky, it is!

What comes from the outside into the brain not only influences what we see but influences the brain cells that do the seeing. However slightly altered, that brain function then alters the way we see the same subject again. To say that a person is color-blind does not mean that the colors change but that something happened within the brain. The brain's capacity is enlarged by virtue of the cells used. Unused cells will die.

In any given moment, in our cortex, we literally make the decision as to what we are going to see.[10]

All of this leads to my thinking about the concept of the field of force in the brain. To me, the field of force is more than a metaphor. The "force" is a part of the dynamic process that we need to take seriously.

In the practical application of science, it is this knowledge that allows for the developing of a chip that can be inserted in the brain whereby an individual can control movement by thinking. This "miracle" first performed in brains of monkeys has now been used successfully in humans.

Similarly, if we who believe in the Holy Spirit follow out the logic of what I am saying, does not the "reciprocal" nature of the brain give a new importance to the Christian view of prayer and meditation?

Scripture, such as the Sermon on the Mount (Matthew 5-7 and Luke 11:13), holds that we do not know how to pray. We in fact need that field of force called "the Holy Spirit" in order to know what and how to pray.

## *The Cerebral Cortex*

We then have the large part of the brain called the cerebral cortex. Dr. Carl York, one of those to whom this book is dedicated, has a helpful suggestion: Think of a tablecloth one would put over a card table. In your mind, pick up the cloth and crumple it into something of a ball.

The crumpled cloth in front of you is about the size of the cerebral cortex.

Now look at the "mound" you have of the tablecloth. The front part is called the **frontal lobe**. In the left hemisphere of this frontal portion, we have what now is identified as the place where we decide things. Some call it the "executive function" of the brain. Other parts here relate to social expectations of what is good and bad. Some of this area influences how we use parts of our body – here strokes cause damage to the use of those parts.

With imaging technology, when the brain works, we see activity in the form of increased collection of blood in the activated area.

In the right hemisphere, this accumulation of blood indicates the presence of heightened emotional activity. It is an oversimplification to say that the left hemisphere then has to decide what to do with the feelings discovered in the right hemisphere. Yet, there is a degree of truth to that observation.

The central and very top part of the brain is called the "**central sulcus**." As one moves down toward the back we have the **parietal lobe** that contains the feeling sensations. Way down toward that little bump we feel in the back of our skull is the **occipital lobe.** That area relates to seeing.

Down and toward the front, again, we have the lobe that deals with hearing, memory, and a sense of self (called the **temporal lobe**). It connects closely with the mid-brain or limbic region we just mentioned.

Key in all of this is a section of tissue that unites the two hemispheres and in many ways pulls the brain together called "the great body" or "**the corpus callosum**." It allows communication back and forth across the two hemispheres of the brain.[11]

### *Meet Michael Faraday*

The person who has both influenced and guided me the most in thinking through this matter of the "field of force" is Michael Faraday.

Faraday's work became basic for people such as Albert Einstein.

The work of this man of several centuries ago has come to mean much to me in these later years of my own life. That work has proven as important to me now as did the writings of the Dane Soren Kierkegaard when I first considered the ministry as a profession.

Faraday it is who first developed the test shown us by R. J. Jungerman in high school.

What is helpful to all of us is that Faraday had respect not only for basic research but also for "philosophical physics." He sought to understand the meaning of research discoveries.

Faraday was a Presbyterian, as am I. That is no great surprise. What does surprise is the fact that Faraday gave leadership to a very conservative group of Presbyterians called Sanenaitans. This group would not allow anyone to be part of the group without being clear as to where that person stood both theologically and scientifically.

What should interest us is the fact that his church faith group had no more trouble with his relating science and faith than he did.

In browsing through publications of Faraday's collected papers, I found the following two quotes:

The Fifteenth Series – Notice of the Character and Direction of the Electric Force of the Gymnotus – Received November 15, Read December 6, 1838.

"1749. Wonderful as are the laws and phenomena of electricity when made evident to us in inorganic or dead matter, their interest can bear scarcely any comparison with that which attaches to the same force when connected with the nervous system and with life; and though the obscurity which for the present surrounds the subject may for the time also veil its importance, every advance in our knowledge of this mighty power in relation to inert things, helps to dissipate that obscurity and to set forth more prominently the surpassing interest of this very high branch of physical philosophy."

Note particularly how he moves from the physical to the biological – that is, to the human nervous system.

And elsewhere in the same collection we find:

Eleventh Series – on Induction -- Received November 30, Read December 21, 1837

"Induction an Action of Contiguous Particles 1161 -- ....to those philosophers who pursue the inquiry zealously yet cautiously, combining experiment with analogy, suspicious of their preconceived notions, paying more respect to a fact than a theory, not too hasty to generalize, and above all things, willing at every step to cross-examine their own opinions, both by reasoning and experiment, no branch of knowledge can afford so fine and ready a   field for discovery as this (i.e. Electricity)."

This particular article goes on to say that electric power does not go from one spot to another without contiguous particles through which that power passes.

That statement fits with those views of the mind which hold that there is no mind without some form of embodiment. The statement also fits with Paul's writing in I Corinthians 15:44 "If there is a physical body there is also a spiritual body." (In fact, the whole of 15:35-55 and the whole of Faraday's lecture have a number of surprising parallels.)

## *The Mind as a Field in Process*

In this connection, then, we must remember that within the brain we have "neurons." In fact we have billions of neurons that share chemical, electronic impulses.

Each neuron is an organic entity in and of itself. Yet these entities do not operate in isolation.

As Descartes and William James and countless others have observed, these many parts operate as one. We think of ourselves as a unity. There is a force that coordinates all of this, and that "force," is what I have called a "field."

Yet not all fields of force operate in exactly the same way.

We must distinguish between a field of force and its process. In the next chapter, I write of *fields* of shame, empathy, and memory and the *process* of forgiveness. In fact, Dr. Richard Restak identifies the mind as a process. He writes "Mind is the name of a process, not a thing."[12] From the work of Tom Farrow, then, we will see that forgiveness is a specific process of the mind that makes use of the different fields of force.

## *The Role of Environment in the Process*

As a German who came to the United States in the 1930s, Kurt Lewin made a dramatic discovery—that field theory applies to interpersonal relations as well as to physical relations.

In his transferring of field theory from physics to the social world in which we all live, Lewin accomplished four results that are critical for the dynamic of forgiveness:

1) He put every individual person and every individual process into the larger context of a community. He spoke of the individual's space.[13] Forgiveness then is a process that relates to the individual space of a person and the space of a group.
   a. This "space" included the community whether or not it was one other person, the experiences of his or her own past life, a family, a faith group, a class at school, a

16

business community, an audience at the theater.

2) He postulated both qualitative and quantitative aspects of phenomenon.[14]

    a. His view fit the view of this book that there is a difference between qualitative and quantitative.

    b. He did not reduce the field just to what could be measured.

3) He developed a mathematical approach.

    a. The attempt is an excellent contribution. However, it goes beyond the realm of this book.

    b. For those who wish to pursue this matter, I express only a concern for the danger in reducing what is qualitative to quantitative formulas. This reductionism destroys the very point being made of a "field of force." We need to build on Lewin's work in a way that does not run the risk of all reductionism.

4) He made the critical distinction between the here and now of any experience and the impact of all past experiences that effect the present but are not the present.

    a. The differentiation between a memory and the effect of that memory is critical. These are two different dynamics even though they are related.

    b. The effect of an overbearing father or an over protective mother may have had one result in childhood, but it has a different result in adulthood. In adulthood, other experiences of life have emerged that result in a memory reaction that is quite different from the original experience itself. If a bully socked me in the school yard, the immediate reaction would be, "that hurts." Later in the day after talking with a friend, the reaction might be, "that was unfair." Much later in life, especially if other bullies have hit me, the reaction may well be "I am worthless or this would not keep happening." Thus, changes in the environment result in neurological changes of the remembered past experience.

This last point has significance for the process of forgiveness. What it means to forgive or be forgiven in the moment of an unfair act is one thing. The matter is quite different, however, when the memory of past hurts is colored by years of other experiences.

The environment about us has far more to do with the development of our brains than some have previously thought. The arguments about the effect of our surroundings and the "way we were born" have gone on for years. It is called the argument between nature and nurture.

During the 1950s, graduate lecturers would say that most of what we are as individuals comes from our genes and our inheritance. However, there is little advantage in arguing about which has the greater influence, the environment or the way we were born. *Both* our genetic make-up and our environments have impact on us.

### *Developmental Process*

One of the lessons of brain studies is that we in fact *do not* have fully formed brains at birth. Instead, we know that our brains develop as we grow. The child psychologist Piaget thought that the brain developed until a child was 12. Recent research suggests that the age is 25. And current work by Professor Richard Davidson of the University of Wisconsin suggests that the mind and experience can influence brain development all our lives. (This controversial statement is reported in a number of articles on the Internet under Dr. Davidson's name and in his research with the Dali Lama – reported both in book form and an article in the *Wall Street Journal* on Friday, January 19, 2007)

Current reports out of the decade of the brain suggest that most of the initial formation of brain cells begins in the uterus during the third and six months of pregnancy. After birth, a process of pruning develops. Those brain cells that are not used disappear. In their place other brain cells form in relation to the environment.[15] Between the ages of six and twelve, the brain neurons grow bushier, "each making dozens of connections to other neuron and creating new pathways for nerve signals." Gender factors play a role in the development as well.

Although it is not yet clear what drives the pruning and the build up, it appears that the death of cells carries right on through the life of any individual. Given the experience of retraining of stroke victims, it is equally clear that some new parts of the brain can be trained or developed even up to the experience of death. The point is that there is, as Lewin suggested, an internal environment and an external environment.

The reality of environmental influence means that the *context* in which we live has strong bearing. Many modern mothers carefully choose the music children hear in the crib. These mothers put more than mobiles over the crib. They periodically flash certain designs before the infant's eyes. These designs stimulate the vision aspects of the brain. This approach takes advantage of that research which suggests that the brain develops from the back forward.

As we move ahead, we will pay more and more attention to the word "context." The "context" of forgiveness has a strong place in the dynamic of forgiveness. These modern mothers have paid close attention to the context in which their infant children grow.

## *The Culture as Part of the Environment*

The context of our personal, internal environment and our cultural, external environment influence each of us.

The internal environment such as brain development just mentioned, memories, feelings, and bacteria sometimes act individually and sometimes interact with the external world.

The influence of our cultural environment shows up in many ways – one of which is the naming of children. (Here, note the work of Catherine Cameron – *The Name Givers*).

I also note the work of Dr. Matthew Erdelyi of New York who calls our attention to the fact of Freud's early attention to the importance of context. Dr. Erdelyi's own thought is seminal in the area of brain studies.

What takes place in something like miscarriages makes the point.

As a pastor, I have had mothers with miscarriages as well as with still-born infants ask me to conduct a burial service for them. The parents had already named each child.

By contrast, in some Asian cultures especially, there are moments called "naming" moments.

One such cultural example comes from a tribe in the Philippines. There, the parents do not consider a child a person until after one year of birth when the child is then given a name. People in such a culture will take a very different attitude to the fetus and its development from those in a culture that even gives a name to an unborn fetus.

When a culture does not recognize the identity of a person until the naming years, how can forgiveness become a factor until an identity is established? The Eastern Orthodox Church recognizes that question when it agrees that a small child may partake of the sacrament of communion. A grown child cannot without having made a full confession.

In this way, we note from brain studies then, an inter-play between the cultural environment and the biological environment, between the environment and the physical brain. All these become part of the process of the development of the brain not only through birth but all ones life. The reality of development in each of us applies also to forgiveness. The experience of forgiveness is not a one time thing. The experience of forgiveness grows, develops, becomes more and more imbedded in us as we develop and practice it.

If the mind is a process that develops, so forgiveness must be a process that develops in the human brain.

## *Who Are We As Persons?*

What we have said leads to the view that we are more than just machines—more than just the product of some creative process. To say that we are a person is to say that we not only are created but that we have the capacity to create what is totally new, totally different.[16]

Long ago in her book *Philosophy in a New Key*, Susan Langer wrote that the difference between us as persons and us as a line in the list of animals is the difference of one day of creation. The gift of language was "the key" that made the difference.

It takes creativity to express oneself in a language and it takes creativity to understand what language communicates.

## *Becoming*

What does it mean to say "We can create something new"?

It means that we have never arrived. We can always create something new and become something new.

Therefore, as the late Gordon Allport expressed it, we are always in the process of becoming.[17]

One may ask, "Becoming what?"

The answer is, "Becoming ourselves."

This process of becoming incorporates earlier stages of our lives into later stages of our lives. In this process, self-awareness plays a large part.

Wrote Allport,

"Personality includes …habits and skills, frames of reference, matters of fact and cultural values, that seldom or never seem  warm and important.  But personality includes what is warm and important also – all regions of our life that we regard as peculiarly ours, and which for the time being I suggest we call the *"proprium"*[18]

Allport notes that we all have a sense of our bodies, a sense of identity, a sense of self-love, a sense of a feeling of involvement with that which is beyond ourselves, a sense of reason, a self-image that is moving into the future, and a sense of meaning.[19]

This proprium is a *force* about which we still have much to learn.

Allport rejected the idea that this force is a little person in our brain as in Descartes. Unlike Descartes' critics, however, Allport did not reject the fact that that "something" is a field of force that brings a "unity of personality." This "unity" is never "the unity of fulfillment, or repose, or of reduced tension." It is the unity of the field of force itself.

## *The Yin-Yang of the field of force*

A critical observation from field theory about the field of force says that every field has two poles – a positive and a negative.

Just as a magnetic field has a positive and negative pole, so we have poles in the "fields" of human relations. As Jung and others have noted in Asian thought, there is a part of the opposite pole in either the negative or positive aspects of a force. The Korean flag itself represents that in its design.

Out of Chinese philosophy there comes the view of the Tao and within the Tao the "yang" and "yin" of all life. This positive-negative, male-female, light-dark of all of life is ever in tension and always in need of being harmonized.

On my desk, I have a picture that shows a young child balancing on a tight rope. The caption reads, "life is a delicate balance." That is very true of the field of force. In the field force that is in each of us, we have a delicate balance between yin and yang.

Yin is not good and yang bad. Both are necessary. Both are part of life.

## *Poles in the Field of Our Life Force*

An initial polarity in the yin-yang of our life force is that of becoming individuals and becoming attached in community. Each individual influences the community just as the community influences each individual.

This creative process is never static. A child begins attachment in the womb of the mother. At birth, the child must become an individual body separate from the mother. As time goes on, the child must develop attachments to mother, father, and the community of siblings.

The psychologist Piaget wrote of how a child develops a morality that suggests how to survive in a group – what goes and what does not. This process fits across community styles – in the gang with its colors and the Scout troop with its codes. As the child grows he or she has to discover himself or herself again and again with the question of who he or she really is. "What do you want to do with your life?" becomes a drive back to the need for identity. The discovered identity may be in sports, a profession, a particular business, or a group of friends.

In each, the attachment develops such that some people cannot separate themselves from their work. One parishioner introduced himself in a group, "I am Union Carbide." In Korea, women often go not by their own names but by the name and work of their husbands. "I am the professor's wife" or "I am the President's daughter" are not just descriptive comments. In Korea, those phrases are standard ways of identification for women.

However, one does not always stay in one spot or with one company or with one husband. A couple separates, a wife dies, and a husband is "killed in action." "Mr. Union Carbide" retired. I do not know what happened to him for he moved to another state. In India, women who become widows have such a loss of identity that care for them becomes a major issue in the culture and in the church.

The importance of this matter of attachment lies at the base of those cultures that do not regard a child as a person until named. Dimensions of this attachment get reflected in rites of attachment such as a bat or bar mitzvah or baptism or confirmation.

In *The Developing Mind,* Dr. Siegel not only speaks of the importance of the first year in forming attachment patterns, but of the effect of those environmental patterns on the development of the brain itself.[20] He joins those who would see levels of attachment as ranging from being attached, to ambivalence about attachment, to avoiding attachment, to being totally disorganized and disoriented.

In her writings on the subject, the late Maxine Plummer of the Presbyterian/St. Luke Medical Center in Denver preferred to see attachments as "healthy," "anxious," "seemingly indifferent," and "primitive."[21]

Whichever view one chooses, it is clear that any one of us have different levels of attachment with different people at different stages of our lives. At whatever stage, these relationships are important to us as we move between the poles of individual identity and being part of another in community – be it marriage, school, a company or a people on a tour bus.

The question then for us in relation to forgiveness is this:

What role does the dynamic of forgiveness play in allowing us to maintain the "delicate balance" between ourselves as individuals and ourselves as "attached"?

A second polarity is the dynamic between being anxious and being at peace.

We are individuals that have, in our brain stem, a fight or flight mechanism that kicks in when we are frightened by a gunshot or a rattlesnake. Anxiety shows the same reaction in our brains as fright except that we do not know what scares us.

A pastor-in-training reported a sense of anxiety whenever he called on a particular older woman in his congregation. In counseling, he suddenly realized that the woman reminded him of a powerful, scary female teacher he had had in grade school. When aware of the connection, he could deal with it.

Again, people often come to church with a sense of foreboding, a tight stomach, or a dry mouth. One woman had a sense of guilt over the care given her aging mother. During a period of silence in the church as the organ played, she realized the source of her anxiety and her mind calmed down. In our concluding chapter, we will speak of how a church liturgy can help. The answer begins with awareness of the process of forgiveness as a process that allows us to become forgiven – and to know that we are forgiven and thus freed of bondage to anxiety.

We usually see the sense of anxiety as a negative. Yet, awareness of being anxious is good in that it sends a signal that something is wrong. The delicate balance between anxiety and peace is important. With the woman just mentioned, the *context* of the music, the sense of being "at home" with that congregation, and the time for integrating the feelings and confessing them (albeit silently), helped. On that occasion, the church liturgy proved to be an *instrument* that allowed for the process to move forward.

A final sense of balance at this point comes when we alternate between a sense of sin, shame, or failure on the one side and a sense of wholeness, peace, and wellness on the other

In the context of a faith group, sin means being cut off from God, from others, and from oneself. Sin is feeling that we have not lived up to what we feel we ought to do. Shame and failure are feelings that alert one to that problem. The question then comes, "What must I do to gain a sense of wholeness or restoration?"

Forgiveness that allows for creativity plays a role in achieving that wholeness. We will look at several examples in the final section of this book.

## *The Poles of Context and Instrumentation*

In all the studies of the brain, a critical dynamic emerges.

That dynamic emerges in two words just mentioned – "context" and "instrument." The dynamic that emerges is different in different cultures. Forgiveness requires a culture that allows for creativity. Forgiveness requires a practice in that culture that brings the creativity to conscious awareness. The "context" and the "instrumentation" are the poles in this creative field of force that grow out of the process and the practice of forgiveness.

In those cultures that do not have the word "forgiveness" in their language, we still can find the process. Therefore, wherever we find that dynamic process, we have what elsewhere is called forgiveness. We have a forgiving dynamic that has a dimension of *letting go* the impact of the failure – whatever that failure is.

Everyone knows the experience of trying something new and suddenly realizing, "I can do that."

So also is the experience of forgiveness. As one tries the practice of forgiveness, what is it that allows the dynamic of creative living to come alive so that we can say, "I've got it; I really am forgiven"? That statement becomes the "instrument" that has made the experience real.

In the chapter on the Bible, we will see these dimensions of context and instrument again and again. In Part II, we will look fully at that dynamic of forgiveness as a process with the poles of context and instrument. We also will ask what it is that mediates the context of forgiveness so that we can see that freeing dimension. I simply call attention to those dimensions.

## *Summary and Next Steps*

Allport in his book *Becoming* said that one must not reduce the life force to the word "soul" as though a little man within us performs some function.[22] Today, countless books emphasize that without a body there is no mind.

I have also emphasized that there is such a thing as incarnation.

Now, as we become aware of field theory and use it is a metaphor, four points emerge:

❖ First is the importance of the perspective from which we look at anything including a "field of force."
❖ Second is the role of a context in which that field of force is

free to operate.

❖ Third is the medium (or mediator) which "incarnates" the field of force – eg. an electric wire.

❖ Fourth is the instrument by which the field force is received and comes alive as a result.

# Chapter Two
## The Fields of Play:

### Shame, Memory, and Empathy

### Introduction

Before we focus on the process of forgiveness itself, we must look at three capacities of the brain. Without the capacity for shame, memory, and empathy, forgiveness cannot release its power.

In our initial picture of the brain, we identified the concept of the field. In the biblical picture of life, we will identify a spiritual dimension called the Holy Spirit. That discussion will identify a cosmic dimension of *field* that has the power of creativity.

In chapter four, we will see the biblical suggestion that the field of shame is itself a force which is basic to the way we react. Let us begin with that field. More than that, we will see that shame is the problem that forgiveness must solve.

In today's world, one almost has to argue the importance of shame. Even so-called "shame cultures" may not speak of it as much as before. Nevertheless, shame is an amazing dynamic that we must face whether we like to label it or not.

We speak of shame also because it has a positive as well as a negative dimension. That is to say, shame has its yin and its yang. Shame in itself is a gift of the way we are created. Shame is also where the blame game starts. A major point of this book is that forgiveness is a better intervention to the issue of shame than is the blame game. Forgiveness as a practice allows us to use both the positive and the negative aspects of shame.

Memory emerges as the next major field of activity. We need to look at the correlation between the dynamic of memory in the brain and the understanding of memory in the Bible. In scripture, sometimes we hear the prayer "remember not" and other times there comes the request, "forget not." For Christians, "do this in remembrance of me" has special meaning

Experience also tells us that if we do not remember something, we hardly can forgive that "something."

From the world of science and counseling as well as the world of the Bible, empathy also takes on special significance. Many biblical references describe the experience of empathy even though they do not use the word itself The comment of the Apostle Paul in Philippians 2:5 is the key example.

That passage speaks of two minds connecting – the mind of Jesus and the mind of any one of us. The actual quote is, "Let the same mind be in you that was in Christ Jesus."

In the section on empathy, we ask, "What actually happens in the biblical reference of Philippians?" Often the words of that chapter get interpreted as a call for humility. That certainly fits. But the real point is God's ability to identify with us, to feel our pain, and to be where we are. That is to say, "God empathizes with us. We should empathize with each other."

In this chapter then, I will try to give data which helps understand how we may use shame, memory, and empathy as tools in releasing the power that is forgiveness – namely the power to be creative.

One more thought by way of introduction: It is in becoming creative that we become truly human – for we return to the way we were ourselves originally meant to be. (Theologically, one would say that we return to our essence as human beings.) To say that we are created in God's image means we are essentially creators. We therefore give a positive meaning to the phrase, "I am only human." We no longer blame our errors on our humanity. Forgiveness thus replaces shame with a capacity to heal, to strengthen ourselves and others, and to find what the Hebrews call, "Shalom."

## *SHAME*

### *Definition*

In the Bible and in the cultures of the world, "shame" has a multitude of definitions. In defining shame, we must remember our opening statement that "shame" is the problem forgiveness must solve.

One of the most accurate and succinct studies of the word occurs in the Dictionary of Pastoral Care and Counseling, (Abingdon, Nashville, 1990,) Carl D. Schneider, PhD at that time on the staff of the Grady Memorial Hospital, Atlanta, Georgia, is the author. The opening line of his article reads:

"SHAME: A painful feeling of being exposed, uncovered unprotected, vulnerable. Etymologically, the indo-European roots from which shame derives mean 'to cover.'"

Dr. Schneider then goes on to describe three forms of shame:

Shame anxiety – a feeling of exposure that will lead to rejection;

Being ashamed – a fear of being perceived as disgraceful;

A sense of shame – a "reaction formation" to defend against offensive behavior

As I speak of it here, "shame" means a feeling that assumes some form of exposure before other individuals or before God. At least one feels a sense of exposure before whatever we perceive as the source of life. This source initially is ones parents. As time goes on, that source becomes a peer group – such as a gang or a team. Later the source may be perceived as a husband or wife or place of employment. Ultimately, people see the source as something greater than us all—for some it is "intelligent design." For other it is "the big bang." For still others, it is an amazing evolutionary force. And some combine dimensions of all three.

All these definitions speak of a "feeling" dimension just as this book on forgiveness also focuses on the dynamic of forgiveness – not just a theory or doctrine.

With regard to the brain, we refer to activity that takes place in both the mid-brain and the cerebral cortex. There is what scientists call a "cognitive" dimension to shame. To feel shame is emotional, but shame is not just emotion.

## *The Generic Problem*

Anthropologist Margaret Mead, once head of the Natural History Museum in New York, used to speak of shame cultures and guilt cultures. In some ways, the distinction still has validity. Yet the distinction now seems too neat.

When I wrote in the 1950s and early 1960s, very few Westerners spoke of shame at all. Along came Donald Nathanson's book *The Many Faces of Shame*, and the situation began to change. John Patton, then of Columbia Theological Seminary in Decatur, Georgia, and others in the field of pastoral psychology, began to speak of shame. Many neglected Nathanson's more profound study entitled *Shame and Pride: Affect, Sex, and the Birth of the Self* (Norton, N. Y. 1992).

Since that basic study, much has emerged on the problem of shame – enough that the dimension of shame in the so-called "guilt culture" of the West cannot be reduced just to issues of guilt and responsibility.

So far as Asian thought is concerned, we find a similar situation but in the reverse direction. As China has begun to develop its new systems of law, the issue of guilt has become part of the Asian culture. The way the law is administered may not be the way westerners would like; but the issue of guilt and innocence still arises.

## *Shame as a Social Experience*

In junior high, a student misspelled his own name. The teacher saw it, pointed out the mistake to the rest of the class and ended by saying, "Aren't you ashamed?" Had the student noticed the error herself, she might have thought, "Wonder how that happened?" If the teacher had mentioned it privately, the student might have thought "that was stupid." Such a feeling is a mild form of shame. When said in the front of the whole class, however, the feeling of shame magnifies.

Silvan Tomkins, in his work on affect, identified shame as being primarily a social phenomenon. The illustration of the student misspelling her name certainly supports his view. Donald Nathanson, in following Tompkins, also lifts up the role of shame as a social experience. In fact, Dr. Nathanson says that one is not ashamed when alone.[23]

Shame-humiliation comes comparatively late in the developmental process. One does not find it in the primitive brain. The emotions generally are found in the mid-brain and in that portion of the mid-

-brain or limbic system located next to the higher association of the cortex that is responsible for thought.

Does this not mean that, from the standpoint of the brain, to have emotions sets apart "higher" species of life from "lower" ones such as a snake or lizard?

The decision as to what to do with those emotions rests in the cerebral cortex. All of this is to say that the "gray matter" of our brain places a higher sense of responsibility, expectation, and ability on humans than on those with less developed cortical areas.

(Legally, this information becomes the basis for a jury acquitting someone because of mental illness or "diminished capacity." In effect, "diminished capacity" means that ones human brain returned to a more primitive state of operation than would be normal – a state that could not have feelings much less awareness of right and wrong.)

The field dimension of shame is shown when we learn that guilt, another form of shame, is on the left side of the brain and that the expressions of guilt (shame) such as facial expressions, come from the right side of the brain. Shame is a field of process that uses several of the brain systems.

In the total dimension of shame, then, we have a field of energy that relates to both hemispheres. In the West we speak of guilt and ones debt to society. The Asian approach leads us to raise the importance of the debt to oneself or ones tribe or ones clan. Seen in the framework of shame, the issue of guilt calls us back again to the matter of how we were created (in the image of God). That brings the matter of shame into awareness not so much of guilt but of our failure to live up to the best that is in us. That in turn speaks of forgiveness as involving our relation to ourselves as well as our relation to other people and to God

Given that the Bible is more an Eastern book than a Western, we should not be surprised that this reframing of the problem sees forgiveness as required to solve issues of both guilt and shame.

## *Positive and Negative Aspects of the Brain*

If shame, as a field of force, has a positive dimension, what is it?

The negative dimension of shame comes when we think poorly of ourselves because of the shame. The positive side of shame tells us that something is wrong. Shame is like a fever that tells us the body is out of balance. Shame is like the capacity to feel the heat of a stove that warns "watch out." Shame gets our attention for reflection, inner assessment, or cleansing and correction.

The negative side of shame can leave us feeling that we are worthless, alone, and no longer part of the community of God. To pick up on the biblical analogy, we have lost paradise.

Professor Pamela Cooper-White has demonstrated the positive and negative in her book *The Cry of Tamar*. The story of Tamar comes in II Samuel, chapter 13. In it, Tamar is forced to "lie" with her brother Amnon. She protested and spoke of her shame, but all to no avail. From the moment of the rape, she went out ashamed, alone, and with all the feelings of being worthless. As suggested above, the shame showed that something was wrong. However, only Tamar knew it.

The members of the family missed the message of shame. They missed the point. Professor Cooper-White notes that Amnon was ultimately killed – but for the wrong reason. He was killed because Absalom did not like him, not because Amnon violated Tamar. The shame of Tamar should have shown Absalom and David that "something was wrong." Instead, her plight served only to make her a foil for the political interests of the men.[24]

The positive and negative flow of the field of shame is such that it has a dynamic profile, not a static, wired profile. Writes Dr. Daniel Siegel of UCLA, "Shame shows an ascending and a descending crescendo in the brain."[25]

## *The Subjectivity of Shame*

This rise and fall in an individual is subjective. In counseling, the response to shame sometimes gets confused with bi-polar or manic depressive feelings. In fact, a premature diagnosis of bi-polar disorder can lead to a missed diagnosis. When the shame feeling is rising or falling, the identification of shame itself becomes part of the healing process. At the point of identification with a skilled counselor, the person in question at least has someone with whom to deal and can then work on what to do about the feeling. Forgiveness as an experience can become the response to shame as an "ascending and descending crescendo."

## *Shame and Depression*

Shame and depression have a relation but are not the same.

One example is a young survivor of the holocaust. This person entered a contest. Let us call her Jean.

Jean did remarkably well for one whose English was a second language. Yet, she became depressed. Under terrorism, there are no near misses. One is either dead or alive. However, attempts to deal with her as though the depression was the whole story failed. Her embarrassment needed attention as well as her "situational depression." The shame needed attention. Attempts to deal with the shame by drugs alone failed. Both her exhaustion (the situation) and her embarrassment (the sense of worth) needed attention. The care of both a psychiatrist and a pastor ultimately helped. Depression and the shame need healing together.

Depression may result from denied anger. Denied anger may lead to an outburst of heavy swearing that results in embarrassment if not outright shame. That type of depression again suggests the need for an interweaving of ones experience of depression and shame.

For that reason, we need care in understanding and helping an individual sort out the causes of either shame or anger and find that which frees one from being bound to either one of them.

## *Shame and Disability*

Disability comes in different forms. An accident, especially the accident of a brain injury, leads to disability. Illness such as polio leads to disability. Brain functions, such as Alzheimer's, stress, fear, or danger lead to physical disability. The advent of aging and reduced ability to do things may lead to shame and a loss of worth.

In each of these situations, the problem lies not so much in needing forgiveness from others, but in forgiving oneself. Fighting the reality of ones reduced capacity uses up energy that makes one even more aggravated than before. Forgiving of oneself releases the power that still remains. Forgiveness of oneself thus becomes a critical tool in the whole dynamic of forgiveness.

## *Dealing with Shame*

I am not familiar with fMRI examinations of shame alone, but there are a good number that deal with depression. There are a number of approaches that deal with either shame or depression or both.

1) Drugs may be taken for shame of depression but drugs are not always appropriate. A drug can give a sense of happiness, but will not deal with the causes of shame.

2) Group affirmation can help. However, a context of care and love that deals with shame may not help with a chemical imbalance – even where that imbalance such as drunkenness may have resulted in people being shunned.

3) Depression itself may cause a sense of shame wherein one feels that he or she is of little worth because of being depressed. The person really needs a balance of change in the environment and change in the medication.

4) Shame may be handled through aggression. One report of atoning for a sister who had a sexual encounter out of wedlock led to a demand that the daughter of the offending man's family be gang raped. That suggestion was made but rejected in the biblical story of Lot in Genesis (Genesis 19).

Yet, in a sense of shame that leads to anger, some men work out the anger by chopping wood, by hitting the golf ball extra hard, or by skiing down a particularly hard hill. Constructive anger management is both appropriate and necessary.

The whole approach of an "eye for an eye and a tooth for a tooth" seen in much modern warfare is an example of an inadequate way to deal with shame. Adequate ways lead to recovery. Again, we may consider forgiveness itself as a replacement for the "blame game." Certainly, the point made by Dr. Tom Farrow and his research sustains forgiveness as a better way of dealing with an affront than many other alternatives. The work of Professor Fred Luskin and others in the U. S. support the point.

## *The Field of Shame*

The field of shame has an environmental pole and an internal pole.

As said above, Nathanson holds that "shame" is basically a public experience – an experience in which the environment notes the worthless act. Otherwise, an individual may feel stupid, but not ashamed. Only when someone discovers the stupid act does one feel ashamed.[26]

However, we must remember that brain studies also show that there is an internal environment that is as strong and real as the external environment. The external environment may be another person, a dangerous animal, something in nature itself. The internal environment comes from memory – from that which the brain has absorbed and made a part of us.

It is this internal environment that is touched by counseling, psychotherapy, penance, meditation, worship, or what some may call "group process." Because of this internal environment, we become aware that the real need is a process that allows one to deal creatively with life and not just reactively. Shame is a tool when it helps us identify what is wrong. Shame helps us realize when we have "missed the mark" either internally or externally.

Since much of the internal environment relates to another field, the field of memory, we now turn to that second key field as another tool.

## *MEMORY*

### *Memory: Part of the Process in the Experience of Forgiveness*

What is memory and how does it work and why is it important?

*Webster's Collegiate Dictionary* of 1953 has a wonderful definition of memory. Memory is "the power, function or act of reproducing and identifying what has been learned or experienced."

Dr. Daniel J. Siegel of the UCLA School of Medicine warns against a too simple definition of memory. He writes,

"A broader definition reads, "M*emory is the way past events affect future functions.*"[27]

In later chapters, we will argue that forgiveness is related to creativity. If that position holds, forgiveness is important whenever something blocks our ability to be creative. Modern brain studies have demonstrated the reality of Freud's insight that some memories are so deep that we do not know that we have them. Until we can bring to mind those memories that block creativity, how can we experience forgiveness or resolution? If indeed we are forgiven and forget it, what do we do to bring that "freedom to be creative" back into play?

I heard the danger of oversimplification when a radio broadcaster recently spoke of the amygdale as the seat of memory. He built a whole news item around that discovery which he found on an AP wire.

Some of his points were well taken. Yet, that same week, an article appeared in the New England *Journal of Medicine.* The article reported that scientists now noted four major centers of memory in the brain. The reduction of memory to a small almond shaped organ in the mid-brain called the amygdale is just too simple.

We must be aware that memory is a process found in every nerve, every neuron in the brain. Memory is not just in the amygdala or the hippocampus. Every neuron has a process whereby it can come to recall a process and repeat it when called upon to do so.

Drug addiction is possible because of what neurons can remember about response to certain chemicals. People under bombardment so learn to respond to the danger that they do not act, they just react to any loud noise – the slamming of a door or the backfiring of a car.

As long ago as 1949, Donald Hebb wrote a book entitled *The Organization of Behavior.* [28] His insight sheds light on this familiar experience of a war veteran. Dr. Hebb noted that when any two cells or systems of cells repeatedly fired together, they became so associated that the activity of the one set off the activity of the other. Further studies showed that some neurons in a relationship became dominant.

Consider what that means in the instance of rape. Two people in love may engage in sexual play with great pleasure. Associated with that pleasure is the sight of the other person, the sound of the other's voice, the tenderness of a touch. When all of this happens within the context of mutual attraction and affection, all goes well. Betray that trust with the violence of rape, however, and the dominance of the violation overrides everything. The violation has such power that it, itself, becomes the dominant factor. For some, especially children, the experience becomes so overpowering that the touch of another, the look of another, or the certain tone of another's voice turn the pleasure into fear, defensiveness, and the need for protection.

Again, in that instance, the capacity to remember leads to the firing of neurons that makes an intimate relationship with another person difficult if not totally impossible unless -- unless we find something that frees us not to react to others but to act creatively and meaningfully.

If forgiveness is a method of dealing with a problem, as Dr. Tom Farrow has suggested, then we need two dynamics: a dynamic that allows us to let go the dominant neuron that causes the distress; a dynamic that lets us recover an even stronger dynamic that allows us to move forward with creativity.

Here, the professions of psychotherapy, social work, pastoral-care (or practical theology) have their contribution to make. Whether one speaks of Sigmund Freud or Carl Jung or Carl Rogers, or Karen Horney or Katharina Schütz Zell of the Reformation, or Mother Teresa in modern India, or ourselves, we need a method that allows us to act creatively. That dynamic method is the process of forgiveness. The process of forgiveness allows us to identify the basic problem, to let it go, and to allow the inner gift of creativity to come forth.

For the first time, I have introduced the term *"pastoral care."*

For now, I define pastoral care simply as a means of care of that inner force of life in each of us that allows us to deal with life creatively. The result is wholeness. Pastoral care is both an individual process and a group process. Group therapy, for example, is as much pastoral care – albeit from a group – as individual counseling.

## *Science Magazine and Memory*

In coming to the subject of memory we get help from the October 15 issue of Science magazine -- 2004. All of us now have access to continuing and excellent studies of memory. This Volume, number 306, contains several studies that I found relevant to forgiveness. The articles identify various types of memory (page 437) as "episodic" and "long term" memory. Although new information continues to emerge about memory, it more and more becomes clear that memory is not in just one location,

Memory becomes a critical part of the dynamic of forgiveness. As said at the beginning of the chapter, if one cannot remember a failure or a mistake or a moment of "missing the mark," what is there to forgive?

One way to deal with such a failure is to block it out. However, from the days of Sigmund Freud, we know that one does not necessarily "block it out." What is repressed may show up in other ways. Much of Freud's early work explained how a "blocked out memory" might show up in some kind of hysteria. It is possible that when Jesus forgave a paralyzed man and then told the man to get up and walk, it was a blocked out shame that caused the hysteria of legs that would not work. (Mark 2:1-13)

Memory also is important for the recall not only of what has gone wrong but what has gone right. (Again, we have a yin and yang dynamic.)

When at the last supper Jesus said, "Do this in remembrance of me," he was saying in part, "remember that you are a forgiven people." Jesus also speaks, in Luke, of not sharing this feast again until at the royal banquet with God in heaven. The "people of God" are part of that banquet.

As a result, there is a place at the beginning of both western and eastern Christian liturgies where the congregation is reminded that "you are forgiven."

## *Memory as a Field*

The work of Gardner Murphy in his research of the 1950s takes us to a level of understanding that we need when we see forgiveness as a field. In his monumental study of that time, Gardner Murphy of the then Menninger Institute in Topeka, Kansas, wrote: "Memory is the function whereby past experience is revived or relived with a more or less definite realization that the present experience is a revival."[29]

As have others, Dr. Murphy warned against too much reductionism in describing memory or personality. He emphasized, for example, that in memory we should not separate memory and emotion, for we remember both and both often go together.[30] More recently, research by Alan B. Sanfey and his colleagues shows that in economic decision-making, the emotional part of decision-making is as important as the cognitive part.[31]

Leslie Ungeleider of the National Institute of Mental Health wrote that "functional brain imaging studies indicate that learning and memory involve many of the same regions of the cortex that process sensory information and control motor output."

As a way of almost underlining a field theory approach to the brain as opposed to a "wiring" image, Dr. Ungeleider went on to say, "The same regions are also engaged during the conscious storage and retrieval of facts and events, but these types of memory also bring into play structures involved in the active maintenance of memories; on line and in the establishment of associative links between the information stored in different sensory areas."[32]

This information suggests that we should see memory as a process of many forces that go on within different regions of the brain. We must then ask the question, "What do we do that allows these forces to accomplish the integrative work of memory?"

The question has risen in research as to whether all memory processes are the same in everything that lives. This question is important, for there are different expressions of memory in every living entity. Professor Feldman of Berkeley speaks of the memory of an amoeba that knows what to do to get food and to reproduce.[33] Individual neurons in any one of us "learn" to respond to certain stimuli in certain ways.

## *Primary Memory*

In that context, Dr. Ungeleider speaks of "primary memory." Primary memory increases in the speed of naming or responding to stimuli that have been seen or heard a second or third time. That process shows up particularly in learning motor skills.

A number of years ago, my wife and I were at opposite ends of the head table at a scientific gathering. The event was formal and took place at the Bohemian Club in San Francisco. As we all settled back to hear the introduction of the main speaker, Margaret pushed her chair back – too far. The back leg of the chair slipped off the platform and she was headed for a nasty if not critical fall.

Without thinking, a man in full tux regalia jumped forward from his chair below the podium, caught Margaret, and lifted her and the chair back onto the platform.

How did he do it? Was it really "without thinking"?

This man was an expert footballer in England (soccer to us in North America). He had so learned to respond to sudden movements and change of direction that he acted "instinctively."

I put the words "without thinking" and "instinctively" in quotes because neither is actually true. His training and practice as a successful player had become so imbedded in his memory field that he bypassed all the preliminaries and acted with speed in a way that saved not a goal being scored but a woman from serious injury or death. The memory field was "primed" so that it could bypass many initial steps and jump directly into action.

As a tool, therefore, that allows us to release the creative power, is it not clear that the discipline of drills makes a difference? In athletics or memorizing great literature, or something as basic as dressing, we have a discipline that allows us to do our work. So also with the disciplined practice of forgiveness: Hibbs law shows up again.

In similar fashion, when the Rev. Ben Weir was taken hostage in Lebanon and imprisoned there, he found himself repeating hymns and scripture passages he had memorized. As with the athlete, Ben had drilled himself so much on those passages that they became a memory tool for him in dealing with his captors. They helped release a power so that he related to his captors creatively.

## *The Biblical View of Memory as a Dynamic*

The most often used Hebrew word for memory or remembrance is "zakar." We see it in Deuteronomy 25:19 "Thou shall blot out the remembrance of them" or Psalm 143:5 "I remember the days of old...I meditate upon the works of your hands."

The Greek translation of "zakar" in the LXX (the Septuagint) uses the same word to describe the plea of the penitent thief who was crucified with Jesus when he says, "Remember me when you come into your kingdom," (Luke 23:42).

In a different mood, a different Greek word appears when Jesus says, "This do in remembrance of me" Luke 22:19. That Greek word in Luke is "mnaomai." According to Liddell and Scott's Greek-English Lexicon, that word carries the meaning of "bringing to mind." Whereas the penitent thief was saying, "Do not forget," Jesus was saying, "recover and bring to mind" this moment.

The Hebrew word, according to the *Theological Dictionary of the Old Testament*, also carries the same meaning – the process of bringing something to the mind. The commentary says "...the verb serves primarily to express an intellectual activity that is relational and personal." It also is often placed with the idea of not forgetting.

Jeremiah 3:16 suggests remembrance as "something that is 'taken to heart.'" Here, "heart" is understood to be an expression for the personality as a whole.[34]

The concept, biblically, is that God is "mindful" of certain persons and turns to them. When God does, we have "a new situation."

"God's remembering is thus an efficacious and creative event."[35]

The matter of salvation history is not critical to this book. What is critical comes with the view of the goal in forgiveness. "Salvation" means wholeness and healing. From the standpoint of personal relations, memory relates to being at one with the past and with the present. Theology usually looks at atonement as being one with God and emphasizes "atoning for past sins." The working of memory, as seen in brain studies, suggests a fuller view of the dynamic than that.

Memory as a dynamic process in the sense of a field of force has to do with good relationships, with being one with God, with a neighbor, and with oneself. In each instance, this oneness allows the freedom to act creatively rather than to play the blame game.

In a moment, we will look at empathy which uses memory. Here, I simply point out the difference between a theology that takes seriously a dynamic process of life and one that shows only structures of belief and ethics.

Further, in Greek, the words for remembering "should not be regarded as an exclusively mental process." "Remembering" is also a process of life. Remembering events of the past become motivation for life in the present and direction in the future. So it is that Timothy is expected to remember the ways of Paul and expected to pass on those ways to every congregation. (I Corinthians 4:17)

We need to think of memory, then, not just as intellectual recollection but as a tool for relating to the past as we act in the present and move into the future. That is to say, memory allows for the process of creativity – of forgiveness.

## *Forgetting and Memory*

A definition of memory also needs to clarify the difference between forgetting and not remembering.

One researcher, a Dr. Alkon, when writing in *Science* tells us that memory has permanence and is not the same as forgetting.

"Forgetting is a physical deterioration of memory which can be forgotten only when the vestiges of the cells and networks are damaged and when they die."[36] Thus, a person with Alzheimer's forgets the short term matters but, in early stages, remembers something of childhood or early years of training.

## *Other Types of Memory*

In his book *The Developing Mind,* Dr. Siegel of UCLA has a long and helpful chapter on memory.  He identifies implicit memory in a child, explicit memory in a two year old, and memory processes that coordinate and integrate what is stored.

In a healthy child, for example, implicit memory prepares a child to know what to expect from parents and how to respond. Insecure children who cannot form the basis of attachment with significant others develop unpredictable responses because the relations are unpredictable.[37] Forgiveness, when experienced, allows for attachment to develop.

In attachment theory, memory has a role that becomes part of the process of forgiveness.

## *The Relation of Learning and Memory*

Both the work of J. Feldman and recent studies of other researchers attest to an interesting relationship between learning and memory.

Both become active on fMRI in the same regions of the cortex.

Francis Crick wrote, "an early discovery was that memory could be stored in a way very different from memory storage in a standard digital computer."[38]  He noted three aspects to the process of memory: putting it into the "net," storing it over time, and retrieving it.  There is no particular work in the "nets" that store the information. The "work" takes place in the process of storage and the process of retrieving.

## *Neurons and Connectors*

Both Professors Crick[39] and Feldman,[40] to say nothing of those who write in the area generally, speak of individual neurons and connectors between neurons.

Neurons have their own individual memories. Professor Feldman particularly would remind us of the amoeba's ability to "know" what to ingest and what to leave alone. The connectors between neurons are liquid chemicals, not wires. A particular type of receptor is called a "glutamate receptor." This receptor works only if it has received the neurotransmitter glutamate in the recent past and if the membrane has moved from a negative voltage to a positive.

To most of us, this all becomes very complicated for remembering in and of itself! Yet most of us are aware that we learn most easily when we can associate new information with other information.

These individual neurons do the same thing. So we end with the fact that memory takes place both in each individual neuron and within certain spaces of the brain that interact with each other.

For example, we see a symbol such as the Star of David, the Cross, or the Crescent. Immediately, other information becomes associated and we have to sort out what associations fit. That sorting will include clarifying the context in which we see them.

At an inter-faith meeting, the context may be one that facilitates trust, empathy, and creative thought.

In a news broadcast or a discussion of the crusades, the reaction may be just the opposite. In such contexts, a defensive emotion or the "fight or flight" emotion may come into play.

As we think of the role of forgiveness and the practice of forgiveness, all these factors have a part.

## *Relevant Points of Interest about Brain Activity*

As we move into the general field of empathy and then the dynamic of forgiveness itself, we must keep in mind several points about brain activity.

Hakwan C. Lau and colleagues write of the "representation of intention" that is prefrontal.[41] Tests indicate that there is evidence of intention that precedes action. For example, a hiker may see a rattle snake. The intention first shown is the determination to survive. Does one run from the snake or kill it? Then one must decide either to get a rock and throw it or to back off. Tests indicate a mille-second of difference in time, but clearly, "intention" has a role in determining what we will do.

I give this example as further evidence of the danger of getting too involved in pinpointing some emotions in just this or that part of the brain. A field concept of memory allows us to cover several parts of the brain. Moreover, if our intention precedes our action, and "intention" is in the cognitive part of the brain that suggests something about the intention of forgiveness.

In another article in *Science*[42] we learn that there is strong activity in the pre-frontal region of the brain that stops the reception of memory – stronger than that of retrieving it. This prefrontal activity is significant as we move to the process of forgiveness. This finding and the finding about intention suggest that the field of forgiveness will include the cognitive or thinking part of the brain.

That information about the difficulty of retrieving information also leads to the question of how we break through that barrier. A partial answer comes out of Brazil. The research from Brazil indicates that part of the issue in recalling memories lies in the fact that we receive old memories in a new time. What we remember must be integrated with the new time in which that memory comes to us. That itself takes time. The old information in the new time may now have a new interpretation. Therefore, part of the way in which we break through the "barrier" of the frontal cortex is simply to be sure we give time and space for the process to play out. Time must be taken to reintegrate past suffering and past forgiving in order that both may be handled in the present.

Ivan Izquierdo and Martin Cammarota[43] write, "It is becoming clear that new memories first required a time dependent consolidation process to ensure their permanence and that recalled remote memories are liable, sometimes necessitating a reconsolidation process to reestablish their permanence."

This statement also suggests the importance of repetition for two reasons: old information may take on new meaning in new situations; information needs to be used in order to be kept (brain cells do die).

In that case, love and care such as reflected in the statement of Jesus, "this do in remembrance of me," become an important part of what theologians call "growth in grace."

This information also is evidence that in the process of forgiveness, we need to take time for all these areas of the field to function. For the "feeling" of forgiveness to be real, we need time for the brain to integrate what goes on. The same point fits the following "thoughts on the hippocampus."

## *Thoughts on the Hippocampus*

The hippocampus is a busy piece of equipment in our brains. It picks up emotions, information, and all sorts of data from what we see, hear, feel, taste and experience.

The hippocampus has the same problem as a computer. It can get overloaded. If it had to store all the memory, it would indeed be in trouble. It could not function – or at least not function with efficiency. Just as sometime we need to clear out data from our computers and our physical bodies, so also with the hippocampus.

Those familiar with the developing role of computers and artificial intelligence have a good model.

First, what gets put into the computer goes on our computer monitor that we all can see. However, not everything can be handled on the "memory" of the monitor. Therefore, we "save" what is written and the material goes into a "file" or place of memory storage. After a while even that gets filled and we have to find some way of getting rid of the material. As I write, my laptop is attached to a "zip disc" that allows for memory storage. I also could "burn" the material into a disc to make room for new material in the computer itself.

Both types of disc represent different parts of the brain where storage may require a process of retrieval that is far deeper than we may think. It takes longer to retrieve material from my Zip disc than from the monitor. I have to find that material and retrieve it.

In the same way, the brain has different places for different levels of memory. Of particular use is what neurologists call the "anterior cingulated cortex." That "cortex" plays a critical role in housing remote memory. According to Professor Siegel of UCLA, this is particularly true of fear conditioning.[44] As with the computer, it may take a longer time to retrieve some aspect of memory than others.

Further, Professor Siegel writes of what he calls the "reverse engineering of the mind." In attachment of a child to a parent, for example, the implicit memory of a child is prepared. In a healthy relationship, the child knows what to expect and how to respond. In an unhealthy relationship, we get the reverse process. The child grows up not knowing how to act, using inappropriate responses, and even acting dangerously. Siegel interestingly calls this a form of "original sin."[45]

The hippocampus, therefore, needs two things that free it from overload. It needs to pass on information that can be stored in other parts of the brain. The hippocampus needs what will free it from bondage to an unhealthy past, so that it can move on creatively with its own work.

These tasks are what we identify as the process of forgiveness.

For long term memory, we need what is called "cognital consolidation." That means: If memory is a tool that allows for the process of forgiveness, we need to take the time to let that "consolidation" take place. Something as simple as proper sleep is an example of using that tool. Yoga and other meditation exercises are further examples.

A simple example of how this works comes from the steps to take in a written exam. Some students look at an exam question and immediately start writing. Others take a moment to close their eyes, absorb the question, center themselves in silence, and then make a short outline as a reminder of the direction for an answer.

After years of teaching, there is much anecdotal evidence that those who allowed for that "cognital consolidation" made better progress than those that did not.

Forgiveness needs this process of consolidation in memory both to know what needs forgiving and to know that the healing is real. Memory needs this process of forgiveness as one means of allowing for the recovery of memory. The context of forgiveness gives the freedom for that consolidation.

## *Memory and Identity*

Erika L. Sanborne has written an autobiographical article that speaks of the role of memory in our sense of identity. Ms. Sanborne herself had memory impairment, later recovered, and then wrote about the experience from the perspective of the one who went through the experience itself. She has a telling line in this currently unpublished report that speaks of the 'ultimate issue of identity."[46]

Ms. Sanborne relates care and prayer to the issue of memory and memories role in identity. It is not for me to report a paper that has yet to be published. I note her work here simply to observe that not only does memory have a role in forgiveness, forgiveness has a role in memory. Feelings of worthlessness can block memory and ones self-image. Throughout this paper I hold that forgiveness is a process that allows for the freedom to be creative. One may ask again, "Creativity for what?" The answer: "Creativity for an identity not only as a person but as a person of worth."

Forgiveness needs this process of consolidation in memory both to know what needs forgiving and to know that the forgiveness is real. Memory itself needs this process of forgiveness as one means of allowing for the recovery of memory.

## *EMPATHY*

Empathy stands out as a subject about which new information emerges regularly.

Studies on empathy in relationship to Buddhist meditation and supported by the Dali Lama have been part of these developments. Those studies indicate activity in different parts of the brain. If nothing else, it becomes clear that Hibbs law about the firing of dominant neurons still holds. Therefore, certain practices of prayer and meditation can become so dominant that they are effective even when in situations other than meditation.

We mentioned earlier how modern studies of the brain verify much that Sigmund Freud wrote–especially the concept of a subconscious, the process of repression, and the reality of internal drives.

Equally, modern studies of the brain verify much written by Carl Rogers. That is especially true when we speak of "empathy." The practice of empathy is a tremendous tool in releasing the power of forgiveness.

Some of us first learned of empathy from those at the Westminster Choir College in Princeton.

Carl Rogers demonstrated empathy in a way few people emulate. He had a capacity to relate to individuals that allowed his "clients" to know that they really were heard. That freed the client to look at issues himself or herself and do his or her own "work" in healing. Consider, for example, the following encounter with a former student:

Rogers: Good morning Jacques, good to see you again.

Jacques: Great to see you Dr Rogers; it has been a long time.

Rogers: Indeed it has, but tell me, how are things really going?

Jacques: Well right now I am under some tension in myself and that makes me question myself and my work.

Rogers: That feels unsettling given the work you are in.

Jacques: (With an inner reaction of, "My God, he really heard me") Yes... very unsettling.

Rogers: Would you like to talk a minute?

Jacques: Indeed I would. Could we sit down?

What happened here?

In the first place, Rogers was not as non-directive as his reputation.

When he met his former student, he had a keen interest. Jacques would not have responded as vulnerably as he did without awareness of the interest from a person he trusted.

From the standpoint of brain activity, that sense of concern clicked in Jacques' brain, allowed for a sense of being in tune, and permitted the honest answer as to how he felt.

Out of that expression of feeling, there clicked in Rogers a feeling that he summarized in the word, "unsettled." That phrase turned out to be a good identification of what was in fact going on in Jacques' brain. As both men worked on responding to the feelings first felt and then put into words, both men really heard each other. Both men felt value in the conversation.

## *The Bible and Empathy*

The Bible is replete with empathetic moments. The Psalms hold continued attraction because of the way they reflect feelings empathetically. We have already identified the hymn in Philippians that speaks of Jesus "emptying" himself and taking our "likeness" as an example of empathy.

It is interesting that Paul even identified this as an act of the mind that we are not only encouraged to have but to take as a discipline. (Philippians 2:5)

And the conclusion of it all reflects the same dynamic. In the Book of Revelation, the vision of the New Jerusalem, the Glory of God in the city is the city's light. "The kings of the earth" and the people of every ethnic group will experience the joy of that light – there will be a corporate empathy. Revelation 21:22-27.

Empathy, then, does more than fit a relationship between two individuals. The field of force released in empathy allows communities to be communities in the "here and now." In communities such as the Columbine school and the Amish town where school members were shot, the empathy reported amongst those who had similar experiences in the tragedy was powerful. The empathy proved powerful enough to make strangers suddenly part of a unifying community.

## *The Dynamic of Empathy*

What then is this field of force that people call "empathy"?

Basically, empathy is a moment when neurons that are firing in the brain of one person call for a firing of those same neurons in the brain of another person This phenomenon is called "theory of mind" or "mentalizing."[47] This phenomenon does not mean that one feels the pain that may have caused the neurons to fire. It does mean that the "affect" caused by "affective" neurons fires in both persons.

For example, shortly after World War II, Stanford University and the University of California met for their annual Big Game. On the opening kick off, a Stanford player caught the ball, made a reasonable return and was tackled. He did not get up. He suffered a head injury. Silence! 80,000 people in that huge stadium sat in concerned silence. None of the crowd felt the pain of the "hit" or of the concussion. All felt the affective feelings of fear, of pain, of death, of how the parents must feel, of how fellow students felt with concern for one of their own, and of disappointment for the injured player who now could not continue the game.

When the stretcher carried the injured man to the ambulance, a strong, sustained, powerful applause of support engulfed all in that place.

What was this applause? In each person, there was a desire to give support, to help, to make right what all knew was impossible to make right. No one else had the physical injury or the specific pain of the injury. Yet all had those neurons firing that expressed the feelings of support, of hope, even of prayer. That is an example of community empathy.

On page 1158 of the article by Luiz Pessos[46], the authors propose that empathy is that observation of another person in a particular emotional state that automatically activates a representation of that state in the observer alone with its associated anatomic and somatic responses.

The example also suggests that empathy refers to moments that relate not just to individuals but groups and crowds. There is thus an environmental dimension to empathy.

In this connection, Luiz Pessos of the Department of Psychology in Brown University reported a test of people who saw the same motion picture. The test was conducted by Hass et al and raised the question,

"Will participants who see a segment of the Clint Eastwood film, 'The Good, the Bad and the Ugly' show any similar reactions in an fMRI?"

The researchers discovered that signals from one brain predicted, on average "the signals of another brain over 25% to 39% of the cortical surface."[48] When one considers all the other things that the cortical surface has to cover, that is a remarkable amount of different brains responding in the same way to particular events

## *Learning to be Empathetic*

How does one learn to be empathetic?

Personally, I have met few people with the ability to respond as empathetically as Carl Rogers.   Even he said that if a counselor achieved true empathy for ten minutes in a fifty minute session, that was a successful interview.

Here, however, memory comes into play.   Dr. David Allen, formerly of Langley Porter in San Francisco, has observed (in private conversation) that a person who had suffered or known illness as a youth would have capacity for such empathy as an adult.

This statement suggests two parts of the empathetic dynamic—

1) That there is such a thing as an internal empathy. If I remember what it felt like to be bedridden, the affective neurons fire without my having to go through being bedridden again.
2) That internal empathy allows one to identify with a similar experience in another.

In both instances, one has to be careful that in being empathetic, one does not impose ones feelings on another.

With that caution, we may recall memories as a template for hearing what the neurons in the brain of another are telling and we are telling them. More is to be learned. Yet what we know is useful in the process of forgiveness.

## *Conclusion*

We have now looked at three fields of force: shame, memory, and empathy.

So much continues to emerge from research in these areas and so much still needs to be learned that humility behooves any who study mental health, the art of caregiving, and the spiritual dimension of life.

We now must ask two questions, "What precisely is this dynamic process of forgiveness that deals with these fields of force? How does all this challenge, support, or be instructive as we look at biblical and everyday experience?" As we now move to an evaluation of experiences in the Bible and case studies form today, we must first find a method that allows us to evaluate those events. To do that, we turn to a short discussion of matters of correlation and of perspective.

After that chapter, I have offered some exercises that relate to the experiences of this section.

# Chapter Three
# Methods of Correlation and Perspective for Scientific Precision

## *Choosing a Methodology*

How do we read the Bible on one hand and the lessons of daily life  on the other?

When two people talk with each other, we generally do not worry about how we understand each other.  We just talk.  Yet, when we talk we actually "read" body language, tones of voice, the context in which statements are made and the means by which we make those statements.

Although we act automatically, we sometimes misread the other person or the other person misreads us.  In marriage counseling, often part of the task is to teach a couple "how to read the signs."

When it comes to what we believe and what we really know from investigation, this matter of "reading the signs" becomes critically important.  As we now bring biblical language into the discussion, we need to ask specifically how to be as objective as possible in reading the signs truthfully. "Hear what I mean and not what I say" does not "cut it."

Therefore, after the introduction to the brain in the last two chapters, and with a look at scripture ahead of us, we need a method on how to read the signs of each. Both cognitive disciplines and theological disciplines help us at this point.

The science of how to read the Bible goes by the name "exegesis." That unusual word means "from the beginning." Biblical exegesis means getting a thought or idea from the point of view of the person or people who wrote out the idea in the first place.

People who live in the world of science have a method for getting that truth. That method is called "the scientific method."

When we want the two disciplines to speak with each other, what method do we use?

## *The Method of Correlation*

Christof Koch, as a scientist, spoke of the method of correlation. When he used the phrase, he spoke of the correlation between the mind and the biological changes in the brain when the mind worked.

No one could think of that question in the way Koch speaks of it had we not developed machines that give an image of brain activity – the CAT Scan for example. Particularly with the fMRI – which means "functional MRI" – we now can see where blood gathers in the brain during certain activities such as fear, remembering, or performing a certain act. We even can see that brain activity in matters of shame, memory, empathy and forgiveness.

As stated in our first chapter, Professor Koch says that there is a *correlation* between what goes on in the mind and where blood brings oxygen to a particular section of the brain. To understand the truth of the brain, we look at where the fMRI shows that there is activity during this or that process of the mind.

A philosophical theologian used the same word, "correlation," in defining the work of theology as a science. The late Paul Tillich spoke of correlation as the task of finding answers to questions raised in everyday life. For example, we read much in the news about whether or not abortion is ever appropriate. Scientific data may help us understand when life does or does not begin, but it does not answer the question of morality. The moral question of whether or not an abortion is legitimate comes when we think in terms of the meaning of life, the ethics of taking a life, and what one believes about life.

Those are theological questions to answer when we have questions of human decision making. The question of abortion is but one. For those of us who are Jewish or Christian or Moslem, those are questions that relate to how we read and understand the Bible.

For our purpose in this book, we have the question, "What is the correlation between the biblical writings and the processes we see in the brain?"

For our purposes, both forms of correlation help.

In the last chapters, we clearly asked what in the brain correlated with forgiveness as described by Dr. Farrow. That question makes use of Professor Koch's concept of correlation. In the next chapter, we will ask how the concept of Holy Spirit correlates with the concept of field. Here, we add Tillich's view of correlation to that of Koch. We also will ask how the Bible correlates with the problem of shame.

## *The Scientific Method*

In any search for objectivity and truth, we also have logic and the help of the syllogism.

The scientific method makes use of the syllogism as a means of thinking through issues of scientific observation. As developed by John Stuart Mill (1826-1873) in the days of the Enlightenment, the syllogism is the model for scientific thinking.

The syllogism has a major premise, a minor premise, and a conclusion. The late John Bennett, an ethicist of the 1940s used the syllogism as a metaphor in understanding matters of ethics and human relationships. In the world of social issues, he identified a major premise, a minor premise, and a mode of action.

The traditional example of the syllogism reads as follows:

All people are mortal.

Socrates was a person.

Therefore, Socrates was mortal.

When applied to social ethics, the example would read:

God is love.

I am created in God's image.

Therefore, I must act in a loving way.

Scientists and theologians use this method. This method applies both to biblical thinkers and to scientific research.

By way of example, Islamic thought and science made genuine contributions in the middle--East before the Enlightenment and modern science in Europe. There was no need for tension between science and faith. Medical science and the concept of the Tao have been at the heart of medical practice and religion in Asia for centuries. Again, there is no tension between science and faith   In the west, Galileo, Michael Faraday, and noble prize winner Charles Townes have found science and religion supportive of each other in their own lives.

## *The Need for Precision*

In following this procedure, I am encouraged by the writing of the cognitive scientist, Prof. J. Feldman of the University of California. I am particularly grateful for his work, *From Molecule to Metaphor: A neural Theory of Language* (MIT Press, Boston, 2006)

Dr. Feldman calls for precision in our thinking. He sees the perspectival method as a means of gaining that precision.

The tension between science and religion comes when we are not precise about the perspective from which one is speaking. More than that, the perspectival method accounts for the fact that no one is totally objective in research. We have to take into account the subjective experience of the researcher. That is one reason Dr. Feldman calls for precision. He uses a form of the "perspectival method" to gain that precision.

## *Jerome Feldman's Unique Contribution to the*

## *Perspectival Concept*

Professor Feldman develops his view of the perspectival concept from his work in linguistics. He gives the example of word learning in a child. In talking about the dynamic experience of learning itself he writes, "*Pushing something, being pushed yourself,* and *watching some pushing that doesn't involve you* directly are quite different experiences."[49] (The italics are mine.) Those different approaches represent his three different perspectives.

Professor Feldman goes on to say, "we refer to these as three different perspectives on experience: the *agent*, the *undergoer*, and the *observer.*"

For our purposes, I have renamed these perspective points as the facilitator, the one facilitated and the observer.

As mentioned, Professor Feldman emphasized the need for precision in any science – including the so-called "soft sciences" such as social work, psychology, and psychotherapy. To that we can add pastoral theology and especially what used to be called "the cure of souls" (old English for "the care of souls.")

To gain that precision, he suggested a method of research that begins with clarifying the perspective from which we look at any issue.

In adapting the approach to the cognitive sciences, Professor Feldman's model suggests a three part division from which we may look at any human experience:

> For precision, we must be clear as to whether or not
> we ourselves speak from
> 1) the perspective of an observer,
> 2) the perspective of the one facilitating the experience, or
> 3) the perspective of the one being facilitated.

Since we know that three people can witness an accident and give three different reports, no one of us can be totally objective. By acknowledging at the outset the influence of the perspectives from which we see an accident or a shooting, we increase the opportunity for objectivity.

As mentioned, the beauty of Professor Feldman's approach lies in how we now can correlate matters of science and matters of spirituality. In following Professor Feldman's approach, we may take a sociological term and ask what that term means in the dynamics of personal or interpersonal life.

This approach then takes a scientific finding and asks what that finding means in describing a dynamic in personal or interpersonal life. We then can ask how the two correlate – in the sense of Koch's definition of correlation.[50]

When translated into a dynamic process of forgiveness, we can talk constructively about the process of forgiveness whether from the point of view of psychology, neuroscience, social psychology, or pastoral psychology.[51]

## *The Perspectival Method and Us*

The perspective from which we see anything determines what anyone sees. Therefore, in looking at scripture or physical processes, we begin with the question of perspective. In German thought, the word "weltenschaung" (world view) expresses this beginning perspective. Whether in science or religion, precision requires that we be clear about the starting point of ourselves and of those we seek to interpret or understand. That starting point is our basic major perspective.

Let us take two specific examples:

1) In the first five books of the Bible, the beginning point says that God created everything. Therefore, when Moses gave the Ten Commandments, he did not begin by stating a rule for living. Rather, he quoted God as saying, "I am the Lord your God who brought you out of the land of Egypt." From that perspective, Moses then went on to list ten middle perspectives such as "do not kill." Any one of those Ten Commandments can be identified as middle perspectives. The concluding action, then, might be a non-proliferation treaty with regard to the development of the atomic bomb, a description of worship, or a guideline for relating to other people.

2) Another example is in the Christian scripture where the Apostle Paul looks at the story of the resurrection. He begins from the point of view that Jesus Christ rose from the dead, and thus that we are all newly created (II Corinthians 5:16).

This statement gives a major perspective different from that of Moses. Yet Paul still puts creation in the hands of God. Therefore Moses and Paul have in common the emphasis on creation  Moses and Paul differ when Paul goes on to speak of a "new creation" in Christ.

    a. For Moses, that difference leads to various middle perspectives such as the Commandments themselves.

    b. For Paul, that difference leads to various middle perspectives such as expressed in the Beatitudes (Matthew 5).

## *A perspective defines ones religion*

*Given the example of the Ten Commandments, I would define religion as the perspective from which a person or a culture make sense out of life(to paraphrase Eric Fromm).*

In that sense, everyone has a religion – including agnostics and atheists. We can speak of the agnostic perspective as easily as the perspective of the Torah or the perspective of the Cross or the perspective of the resurrection, or the perspective of the "Big Bang" theory.

How can anyone say, "everyone has a religion?"

Long ago, the social psychologist Erich Fromm spoke of what he called a person's "frame of orientation." (See his *Psychotherapy and Religion*, 1950, Yale University Press, New Haven.) A person's perspective is the frame of orientation from which any of us make sense out of life. A culture's frame of orientation does the same thing.

Unfortunately, a person's or a culture's frame of orientation – the way they make sense out of life – is so important that people fight to the death for the right to hold a particular perspective – be it Islamic, Buddhist, Jewish, Christian, or atheistic. That is why we have religious wars.

Because such a frame of orientation has that importance, in the United States, we insist on freedom of religious expression.

The positive side of a frame of orientation – a major perspective – is that once understood, we can learn from each. When we understand the other person's perspective, it helps us see what the other person sees – whether or not we agree with that person's starting point or conclusion.

The scientist who looks for truth from the perspective of a measurable piece of information can still teach me something even though I believe that there are other ways to look at that same information. I can look at that same information from the standpoint of spiritual reality.

Current literature of both science and theology has ways of making sense out of life from different perspectives.

That statement follows logically from Eric Fromm's view that everyone has a frame of orientation. The statement holds true for a scientist such as Dr. Arbib and the philosopher Daniel Dennett as for anyone else.

## *Perspectives Change*

Something else about perspectives: our perspectives do change.

The more we live the more data we have to integrate into our very being. The more information we have, the more we deepen our understanding of our perspective or even change our perspective. As one person put it in the Gospel story, "Once I was blind, but now I see."(John 9:25).

Somewhere in his early forties, a colleague had a dream that he was in grade school and playing baseball. He dreamt that he hit the ball and began running the bases backward—from home to third to second to first. Such changes had come in his life that he had to go back to the beginning in order to integrate everything again.

That story is an example of speaking as a child when one is a child but needing to put away childish things as an adult (I Corinthians 13:11).

Allport's view of always "becoming" a person helps at this point. Everything, either of science or of faith, must be reintegrated as an adult and in adult terms. Given that reintegration, ones major perspective or world view sharpens. The sharpened perspective brings to conscious awareness precisely the influence of that change on everything else one person thinks or does.

From our first chapter, we know that there is a correlation in the brain with every perspective and every change of perspective. The same event may be looked at from different perspectives and both be true!

## *Perspectives of East and West*

When my wife and I first went to China, we ran into the reality of that seeming contradiction – that the same event, seen from two perspectives, may both be true.

In Xian, I mentioned to a local pastor that his service of worship had no place for what is called, "the confession of sin." As a result, the service had no place to affirm forgiveness of sin.

The pastor of the church pointed out that Westerners tend to look at sin from the perspective of Roman law. He noted that for us westerners, key words were guilt and forgiveness. For the Asian, he said, the key words were "freedom and harmony."

I was struck by the comment. The biblical words for guilt and forgiveness have been understood in the West in the context of a court of law. The experiences of guilt, shame, unworthiness, or "missing the mark" (the Greek word for "sin") are paramount. For those in Asia, however, the key words centered on harmony, balance, and the proper relation between the yin and yang of life.

How we understand the dynamic of forgiveness then depends on the cultural perspective we bring to it. As our perspectives change or as they broaden – we change and our brains change.

In the exchange with the Chinese pastor, had I not been able to grasp the difference in the cultural perspectives and move back and forth between the Asian and the Western, the Asian pastor and I would have had no basis for communication.

Now, today, with my renewed awareness of field theory and its positive and negative poles, I find new meaning in the "yin" and "yang" of Asian thought. An understanding of the cultural perspective makes the difference.

The discussion with the pastor also reminded me of something in my research of years ago. In my research for the book on forgiveness in the 1960s, I wrote of everyone needing an "instrument" that helps make real the experience of forgiveness. In a given choice of phrases, when asked how people would describe the feeling of being forgiven, most marked the phrase, "I feel a sense of freedom."[52] In terms of what made forgiveness real, we found a positive correlation between that which grew out of the Asian perspective and that which grew out of the western experience.

## Conclusion

Out of all this discussion of evaluative research, we have a basis for looking at forgiveness. Not from linguistics as with Professor Feldman, but from personality studies in general, Seward Hiltner introduced the concept of perspectival thinking at the University of Chicago in 1953. He identified three perspectives – communicating, organizing, and shepherding.

In fact, over the years, different people, including me, have identified several different points of perspective from which to look at human relations. Because of his refinement of the process in the cognitive sciences, I have adopted Professor Feldman's approach here. I have changed the labels to fit what appears particularly appropriate for both biblical and interpersonal work.

# Suggested Exercises In Self-awareness

1) Awareness of shame.
    a. Close your eyes and imagine some event in the last day that you wish you could take back – you wish had not happened.
    b. Make a note on a paper of that event of how in that moment you did not live up to what you felt you ought to be – did not live up to your best self.
    c. Simply note in writing or for your remembrance what that felt like – did you want to deny it; run from it? Did you feel flushed in your face, strange in your stomach? Did you find that the awareness of this lead to other times you felt shame?
2) Awareness of memory:
    a. Close your eyes and imagine the most beautiful sight – the place where you find peace.
    b. Imagine a place with a gate – perhaps an entrance to a forest, a garden, or a tunnel through a mountain.
    c. Imagine yourself on a magic carpet as you float through the gate.
    d. Notice signs of the years as you go back further and further in the years of your life to your earliest memory.
    e. What is your earliest memory?
    f. How do you feel about your earliest memory?
3) Self-awareness of another.—an inter-subjective experience.

    a.  In a group, gather in a circle of four or five.

    b.  In the group, lift up a topic of controversy or strong emotion such as: what it felt like to see the planes crash into the world trade center; what it felt like to see a picture of the holocaust victims in a concentration camp; or what it feels like to see bombings of civilians in the Middle East.

    c.  Let one person express his or her feelings.

    d.  After that, let another person respond – but respond by first reflecting to the prior speaker what the other was saying.

    e.  When that prior speaker confirms the interpretation, then the respondent may move on to add her or his comments to the discussion. This process is then repeated around the circle of the group.

4) Self-awareness of forgiveness

    a.  Identify a time when you really felt forgiven—found resolution of a conflict and a healing that freed in you the power to be creative.

    b.  What did it feel like?

    c.  Identify a time when you could not forgive another.

    d.  What did that feel like?

    e.  Ask yourself, "can I live with that feeling or not; why and why not?"

# Part Two

## *Abstract*

In this section, we apply the information on the brain and the methods of correlation and perspective to the Bible and to human experiences. In both cases, we seek to identify what it takes for the process of forgiveness to come alive – whether that process takes place in the one who needs forgiveness or the one who needs to offer it.

Buttressed by neurological information, this chapter lifts up a process of forgiveness that goes from context to mediation of the context to instrumentation or action that makes the context real.

# Chapter Four
## The Bible and Forgiveness

### Preliminary Thought

The concept of creation holds as important a place in the biblical understanding of forgiveness as the concept of a field of force holds in physics.

Our metaphorical use of field theory applied from physics to brain studies meant that we looked at the mind *and* at forgiveness as a process. In the Bible, we now see forgiveness as a process that leads to a capacity for creativity. In this chapter, we see forgiveness not as some fanciful or unrealistic "nice guy" act, but as a tough discipline that releases a power for dealing with life tensions and failures. In the Bible, see the power to live creatively as another way of speaking about the power and the practice of forgiveness.

In order to understand this power as presented in the Bible, we will discuss some correlations between the brain and biblical thinking. To do so, we follow the method for looking at the Bible that correlates with Professor Feldman's method from the cognitive sciences. The method is perspectival. Awareness of perspectives helps us gain precision in relating human relations, the brain, and the lessons of scripture.

## *Biblical Perspectives*

When it comes to looking at any scripture, then – the Koran, the Bhagavad-Gita, the Torah, the Gospels, and on – we need to ask about the perspectives from which each was written.

In the Hebrew and Christian Scriptures, we must take seriously the differences in perspectives behind different parts of the Bible. These differences will enrich our own understanding as we look at them and bring them together for our day as the early church did for its day.

To catch the differences in the Bible, we begin with the fact that the Torah, the Prophets, and the Sacred Writings used in the Hebrew services of worship covered centuries in their writing. The perspective of those in exile who wanted to make sure that people would not forget the commandments was different from the perspective of the ones who wrote down those commandments at the outset.

The book of Deuteronomy comes from the time of renewal in the sixth century before the Common Era (under King Josiah) and the book of Exodus comes from a different time. Therefore, we should not be surprised that comparison of the two books shows differences in perspectives.

Note, for example, the location of the Commandments in the Book of Exodus and the location of the same passages in Deuteronomy: In Exodus, the Commandments appear in the twentieth chapter. In Deuteronomy the Commandments appear in the fifth chapter. These differences in location reflect differences in perspective.

## *Biblical Perspectives of Terror*

In his valedictory address upon retiring as Professor of Old Testament at San Francisco Theological Seminary, Dr. Marvin L. Chaney spoke of the perspective in some passages of the Hebrew Bible as the perspective of "Terror on Every Side."

Thus Professor Chaney sees part of the Book of Exodus as saying that the antidote for terror is being sure that you begin with God. According to Professor Chaney, the antidote for state terror comes in recognizing that it is more important to fear God than to fear the king!

In Deuteronomy, the issue of terror was not as great as the need for reform. Therefore, the task of Deuteronomy was to get the centrality of God and ancient history before the readers quickly. The book puts the Ten Commandments in chapter 5 and then had the rest of the time to spell out what life should look like under a reformed reading of the law.

## *Key Christian Perspectives*

For the purposes of getting at the historic Christian contribution to the dynamic of forgiveness, we begin with focus on the stories of the death and resurrection of Jesus. Each account of the Gospel has a different approach to the story of the death and resurrection of Christ. The Apostle Paul has a still different approach.

When we remember that no one would have written about Jesus apart from the resurrection, the resurrection stories give us a sense of the perspective from which each person wrote. When we ask what the perspectives were, we can identify at least five in the New Testament.

Mark, the first of the accounts, suggests a perspective of awe and fear. There have been other additions to the conclusion of the Gospel

According to Mark. These stories brought the Gospel account in line with other accounts; but they miss the essence of Mark.

The first major miracle in Mark comes in chapter two. There, Jesus heals a man who could not walk. The story ends with the words, "we never saw anything like this." From the beginning to the end, Mark tells the story not so much of what Jesus said but of what he did. Why? We may legitimately suggest that Mark is spelling out the story of something that "no one ever saw like this." That certainly is true of his record of the empty tomb.

In the Gospel according to Matthew, we get the message of the new mediator. In Exodus and Deuteronomy, Moses fulfilled the function of the mediator through whom the message came – keep the Torah ever before you and study it day and night. Deuteronomy expresses that thought by saying, "These things command and teach...."

As Moses received messages on a mountain, so the fifth chapter of Matthew gives us a "Sermon on the Mount." And the last words of the Gospel say, "I shall be with you always, even to the end of the age." Whereas in the Torah, the law as from Moses was important, in Matthew, it is the person of Christ that is the new "frame of orientation." He is the one who will be "with you to the end of the age."

In Luke, a look at the resurrection story on the road to Emmaus speaks of two men who said, "Were not our hearts burning within while he was talking to us on the road?" (Luke 24:32, in the NRSV) Here, the resurrection gives a sense of the real presence of God. (Those who stand in the tradition of John Calvin look at the sacrament as a moment of the "real presence.") In the Gospel according to Luke, we also have that presence in the angel with Mary, in Jesus with the woman at the well, and in the passage on prayer (Luke 11:1-13). In the latter, the promise of prayer is not the gift of what we want but the gift of the "Spirit" – i.e. of the real presence of God.

Both in the Gospel according to John and the thinking of the Apostle Paul, the emphasis is on creation.

So far as we know, the Gospel according to John was written later than the other three. This account gives some stories, but even more, this account gives what might be called "think pieces."

The first version of the Gospel according to John gives the perspective from which we should look at the issue of forgiveness. That perspective is, again, creation. It is this perspective that ties the Christian Scripture to the Torah and especially Genesis.

Just because John is a "Gospel" does not mean that he either says the same things as the other Gospel writers or has their perspectives. John's Gospel had in mind an audience different from the others. Therefore, he had a different perspective from those of the first three accounts (Matthew, Mark, and Luke).

More than that, Herman Waetjen has proposed that the Gospel According to John itself reflects two editors – and thus two different perspectives. His book, *The Gospel of The Beloved Disciple* (T&T Clark, London, 2005) has a sub-title, "A work in two editions." If one follows out the logic of those two editions, it becomes clear that each "edition" represents a different perspective.

## *The Biblical Perspective of Creation*

Of particular importance for our thinking about forgiveness is to look at how the whole Bible begins and ends. The Bible begins with creation in Genesis and ends with a new creation (specifically a New Jerusalem) in the Book of Revelation.

In Genesis 1:1, the Hebrew reads, "Barashith bara elohim" – literally, "In the beginning created God…." The traditional King James begins, "In the beginning, God created the heavens and the earth…" It makes little difference which of these or any other translations one picks. The point is simply this: *creation* is the initial perspective from which the Bible speaks.

The *Holy Qur'an* begins at a different place. It begins with the issue of the oneness of God who is the "Lord of the universe" and what it means both to believe in and to follow Allah.[53]

Genesis begins with creation. The Hebrew word for creation in the quotation above is "bara." That word lifts up what we have "In the beginning."

Of further interest is the view that Genesis 1 appears to have been written in the period of the exile or the immediate post-exilic time (444 B.C.E.) by what is called the "Priestly" group. This information means that the perspective from which this passage is written is the perspective of a people having had to deal with the terror of life in exile. These people were trying to make sense out of that life. In going back to Moses, with the writing of Deuteronomy (the second telling of the law – the Ten Commandments), they brought a highly sophisticated understanding of God and of "how it all began."

In those desperate periods of the exile and then the return to Jerusalem when all had to be rebuilt, the rebuilding began by taking the time for people to get back to their roots. The issue at the beginning was creation. The time of rest (the seventh day) was a time for wholeness (a Sabbath). That Sabbath rest allowed for integration in ones soul of all that had been done. It was a time of renewal, not just a time of worship. The day of rest went beyond recognition of the work of creation and the Creator. The day of rest allowed for integrating the creativity that has taken place in rebuilding the city.

We see the importance of that integration in the writings of the prophets Ezra and Nehemiah. There, we see that the first issue was to build, to create a wall for defense and a city for living. In order to have both defense and life, what did the people do daily?

They worshiped.

The people focused on the source of creation – God.

Therefore, the book of Ezra tells of getting started with the worship of God and then of returning to that center again and again in daily life. The God who created was the center of their attention.

This focus suggests that there are various types of perspectives or perspective points. We can identify the human perspectives we may have as children, adults, people who are tired, people who are joyous, and so on. We can also, however, identify an overarching, *cosmic perspective.* In the life of the Hebrews, this cosmic dimension had to be refined in what might be called "good worship" as opposed to "bad worship."

"Good worship" releases the creative power of God. "Bad worship" gets in the way of the creative power of God  In the book of Nehemiah, that worship of God got sufficiently refined that the people moved from just ritual sacrifices to reading the Torah itself– the book of the law (Nehemiah 8:1 ff).

As we read Ezra and Nehemiah, we find that something happens to the community of faith. We find the people struggling to find their focus, their perspective, in God. We find people being creative themselves in building both a wall and a place for worship. The wall protected them. The place of worship helped them keep their orientation with the creative power called God. That goal is one reason we find people in scripture looking again and again at the Torah which begins with the matter of God's creation.

In Ezra and Nehemiah, then, we see the capacity of a people for being creative and we see worship as having a role in sensing that creativity.

## *Creation As the Starting Point in John*

To see this focus on creation in the development of the early Christian communities of faith, look again at John. The concept of creation as the starting point carries on in the Gospel according to John. The flow of thought moves from the original creation to loss of that creation to a healing that overcomes the loss. John prepares us to see what the new creation will be like because of the Christ

The fact that the Gospel according to John appears some years later than the other accounts indicates a difference in mood between John and the other three – Matthew, Mark, and Luke. (Again, note the work by Herman Waetjen.)

Rather than just getting out the story as did Mark, Matthew, and Luke, John comes to us as both a story and as a reflection on the meaning of the story. John is strong on the "reflection" of meaning. The first words in the Gospel according to John begin with the first words of Genesis: "in the beginning." Both speak of creation. John speaks of the "Word" in the beginning: "In the beginning was the Word…"

The Greek word for "Word" is "logos." We get that in many other words such as "biology" or "psychology" or "theology." The English translation of logos as "word," however, is not the best translation.

The word "logos" has two chief meanings: thinking and speaking. In this word, "logos," speech and understanding become one. The Chinese use the word "Tao" – or "Dao" as it is pronounced--for their translation of "logos." Most English translations of Tao use the word "way." To the Chinese, however, "Tao" also carries the sense of both thinking and speaking. In fact, so much closer are the Chinese and the Greek to each other that the Chinese Bible reads, "In the beginning was the Tao, … and the Tao became flesh." (For a full discussion of the similarity between "logos" and "Tao," I commend the book by Dr Zhang entitled, *The Tao and the Logos,* 1992, Duke University Press).

The prologue of John then goes on to see creativity as part of the grace of God as expressed in the forgiveness of God.

## *Creativity in Paul*

Although we will look at the Greek words for forgiveness, Paul is of interest because he seldom uses those words. Instead he speaks of being "in Christ." I mentioned earlier Paul's statement , "If anyone is in Christ, there is a new creation: everything old has passed away; see everything has become new." (II Corinthians 5:17)

For Paul, that newness may be expressed in different ways. It may be shown in reconciliation. It may be expressed in the choice of a new vocation. It may be expressed in need for a retreat. The expression of this new creation has many applications.

For the purpose of understanding forgiveness, at this point we have again the relation between creation and healing, creation and forgiveness.

## *Creation for What?*

Here, we must raise the question, "Creation for what?" Creation had a purpose. The issue was not just creation in itself but creation that related to healing and wholeness. In Genesis that meant bringing order out of chaos. Elsewhere creation means the wholeness of a people (Isaiah 6), or healing (Mark 2), or restored relations and the end of sin (Revelation 22).

For us living today, the question is, "How do we find wholeness in the midst of the horrors of the day?" In some places that "horror" is like the ancient "terror on every side." For those of us not in war zones or centers of murder, the horror comes from observing those areas on TV or in the press.

How do we get this power to be creative in spite of that horror of terror? For the Hebrews, the question was similar. We need to do for our day something that meets the needs of our time even as the Hebrews did something for the needs of their time.

The German biblical theologian, Gerhard von Rad, puts it well for us when he writes, "Faith in creation is neither the basis nor the goal of the declarations in Genesis Chapters 1 and 2. Rather, the position of both the Yahwist and the Priestly document is basically faith in salvation and election."[54] The experience of forgiveness becomes the experience that releases the power of that salvation.

From that observation, then, we identify the cosmic perspective as the perspective of God as the Creator. We see the goal of worship as that of wholeness, salvation, or peace with God and each other. We find that the process of forgiveness opens the power for reaching that goal.

## *The Perspective of Psalm 51*

To solidify this point in relation to forgiveness, consider Psalm 51.

This Psalm is traditionally identified with King David at a time when he took advantage of his power to get "the woman he loved." The woman's name was Bathsheba. Bathsheba had a husband named Uriah. David ordered that Uriah stand in the front lines of battle where he would be killed. He was killed. That freed David to marry Bathsheba. Tradition says that when the prophet Nathan pointed out the crime he had committed, David repented and wrote this Psalm.

Psalm 51 uses the technical words that describe forgiveness when it begins, "Have mercy on me, O God, according to your steadfast love; according to your abundant mercy blot out my transgressions."

Without using the word forgiveness, these and the succeeding verses ask for all that is involved in the process of forgiveness. And then in verse ten we read, "Create in me a clean heart, O God…."

In that line, we have one of the few places that the word in Genesis (bara) is used--used in a way that brings to the heart of our personal experience the initial power of all creation. What greater evidence that in forgiveness we have a sense of more than just freedom from guilt? In forgiveness, we have the power for creative restoration.

## *An Example for Isaiah*

One other evidence for the relation to creativity comes in Isaiah, Chapters 42 to 48. There, we find other examples of this basic concept of God's creation as distinct from words that refer to human creations of something like art or a good meal.

## *The Goal: A Healed Creation*

In a similar vein, we find the connection between healing and creation in the concluding chapters of the Christian Bible.

The Book of Revelation has its own picture of the New Creation -- a picture that also identifies the reason for this creation. In this book we read, "I saw a new heaven and a new earth; for the first heaven and the first earth had passed away, and the sea was no more." (Revelation 21:1-2) Further on we read, "Then the angel showed me the river of the water of life, bright as crystal, flowing from the throne of God and of the Lamb, through the middle of the street of the city. On either side of the river, is the tree of life with its twelve kinds of fruit, producing its fruit each month: and the leaves of the tree are for the healing of the nations." Revelation 22:1-2)

In that concluding book, creativity and healing come together. The connection is complete – the Bible begins and ends with creation. The purpose of creation is a healing of what has gone wrong – salvation.

## *Field Theory and the Bible*

With this background, we now must ask how the Bible and field theory correlate. Further, how does that correlation influence the question, "Where does forgiveness fit?"

To look for that correlation, we pick up again with the insight of Wolfghart Pannenberg. Prof. Pannenberg is concerned with the fact that an early Christian writer named Origen chose to interpret John's statement, "God is Spirit" with the Greek word "nous." That Greek word can easily be translated as "mind."

For Pannenberg, that leads to understanding "the spirit" as a form of thought or the mind. To do justice to the qualitative difference of the field of force and just thought, Pannenberg would argue that we cannot reduce the "life force" just to reasoning or thinking. The great philosophers like Plato and Aristotle, may have done that, but the Bible does not.

Dr. Pannenberg writes, "The field theories of modern physics no longer view field phenomena as bodily entities but see them as independent of matter and defined only by their relations to space or space-time." For Pannenberg, biblical statements about the Spirit of God are closer to Michael Faraday's idea of a universal force field than to the concept of "nous" or the capacity to think.[55]

Therefore, when we think of the Spirit of God "brooding" upon the chaos described in Geneses 1, the creation comes from a spiritual force field. That field of force is better described by the Greek word "pneuma" than by the idea of a great thought or a great mind. The original creativity is a capacity, *a life force* qualitatively different from anything else.

When then we speak of men and women in God's image, we think of them not just as endowed with minds and sophisticated technology of the brain – i.e. not just super computers. Instead, we think of each of us as having *a field of force*. The physical attributes of that field are manifestations of us and are measurable. In line with the first chapter, the physical attributes *are not* the whole of our being.

## *The Field of Force and the Holy Spirit*

The value of this correlation between a scientific field of force and the Bible's concept of the Spirit is necessary if we are to understand the dynamic of forgiveness itself.

At the outset, awareness of the "field of force" gets us away from just a western view of forgiveness as in relation to law and puts us into seeing forgiveness for what it is: a universal relation to creation itself.

Further, field theory then leads to the question, "what went wrong?" What happened that all this paradise in the original creation became the mess we have today?

## *Field Theory, Yahweh and Us*

Let us return to the second Chapter of Genesis and the use of the word, "Yahweh."

The second chapter of Genesis is a more personal story than the first chapter. Much has been written about the word "Yahweh." The paradise narrative has all the characteristics of a story passed down for many generations. Any who have studied Hebrew know that on the one hand the word God was never to be used because to reduce God to a word was to betray the reality of God. As the *Tao Te Ching* reads in its first line, "The Name that can be named" is not the eternal Name.[56]

It also should be noted that the Hebrew letters for Yahweh (UHAWH) are also the same letters for the verb "to be" or for just being.

What we have then in the second chapter or the Yahweh document gives a second creative narrative to answer the question "What went wrong and why?" If Genesis 1 centers on the "Who" of creation, the second chapter centers on the "us" of creation. The chapter seeks to spell out an answer to the question of "what went wrong" or "how did we humans go wrong?"

Christian theology generally refers to the Adam and Eve narrative as "the fall." Historically, the story tells us that God had a process for the way things should go if they went right. "We humans" failed in that process. "Disobedience" generally describes "what went wrong." Given our discussion of perspective, disobedience took a definite form. Disobedience took the form of humans seeing themselves as the creators of the universe and not a result of that creation. Therefore, what was to be a cosmic perspective got reduced to the perspective of human desires, thoughts, and feelings.

The question of the truth or falsity of this story in history too easily distracts people from its meaning. People ask, "Is it true or is it mythological?" Although interesting, that question is not key. The real question is, "Why do we have the story in the first place?"

The first thing that happens in the story is that Yahweh sets up a process for life. We have two people–male and female. Asian thought agrees and says, "Yes, we have the yin and the yang." These two people are given stewardship of the land and all that lives in land or sea. A certain process is to be followed that involves naming and avoidance–naming of all that grows and avoidance of a particular tree that will fool people into thinking that they are the Creator and not the created.

In that context, Adam and Eve ruined the process.

They ruined it by acting as though they were God and thus changed the process that allowed for their creative living. They did this by disobeying God, and they did it by not taking responsibility for what they did. The disobeying of God is obvious – they simply ate what they were told not to eat.

When they ate, Adam and Eve lost the cosmic perspective. They reduced the perspective to a narrow level. They saw themselves as the center of the universe and not as created human beings dependent on the Creator.

That same problem exists as the great sin of today.

## *The Bible and the Blame Game*

The second insight of Scripture may not be as obvious as the first; but it is just as real. *Adam and Eve blamed others for what they did.* They could not take responsibility.

Adam blamed Eve. Eve blamed the serpent. The blame game has stood in the way of human relations and spiritual relations ever since. Adam and Eve lost the creativity that it took to live in Paradise, and they were sent out to create life on their own. This failure was called sin. This process of rebellion – the blame game – remained the process of people throughout the Bible and does so even to this day.

"Sin" is not an act but a process of being separated from God and from each other. Death emerged as the result of both failed relationships. One son, Cain, killed the other son, Abel. The rest of the Bible speaks of the dysfunctional family, the dysfunctional world, and the dysfunctional religions that resulted.

"What happened?" We lost creative ability. Something was needed to restore that creative ability. What stood in the way of regaining that ability? According to the story, the feeling of shame stood in the way. Genesis 2:25 reads, "And the man and his wife were both naked, and were not ashamed."

After their disobedience in eating the forbidden fruit, they became self-conscious about their nakedness and put on clothes. Genesis 3:10 has Adam explaining to God that he had hidden himself because he was afraid.

Shame has been described as not being what one knows he or she should be. Donald Nathanson writes in his foundational study of shame, "Shame seems always to involve a more or less sudden decrease in self-esteem."[57] Surely that was true of Adam and Eve. Shame got in the way of creative living.

## *The Bible and Forgiveness as a Healing Cure and a Process*

What then is the cure? What frees us to live creatively?

The biblical response is "forgiveness." Forgiveness as an experience is that dynamic in which we become free from bondage to shame that prevents our action. We saw it in Psalm 51. We see it in life all about us. Fear comes from this sense of inadequacy – from the feeling that we can never measure up. Thus a child says when asked, "Why didn't you say something" often replies "I was afraid."

Of what is one afraid?

The child is afraid that he or she cannot live up to expectations that satisfy adults. In a deep sense, that child in all of us has the same reaction at the age of eighty as at the age of eight. We all fear rejection.

In Adam and Eve, the reaction of fight or flight seen in the reptilian brain resulted in the flight to a place of hiding – and ultimately being expelled from the garden. The answer of a "new creation" in the book of Revelation puts us back in the garden with the healing trees.

This discussion leads us, then, to the following questions in this dialogue with the Bible – what is the dynamic of this forgiveness that frees us to be creative and does this fit in all situations?

## *The Forgiveness as a Weight Lifted*

The process of forgiveness feels as though a weight has been lifted from ones back.

From Genesis on through the prophets and the sacred writings, the word most often used to express forgiveness is "a weight lifted." The Hebrew "shalach" has the primary sense of "lightness" or "lifting up."[58]In the Greek translation of the Hebrew Testament (called the "Septuagint") the word used is "remit" or "take away." [59]

The whole picture is caught in John Bunyan's *Pilgrim's Progress*. There, Pilgrim climbs the side of a hill. He carries a great weight of sins on his back. As he gets toward the top, he sees the words, "your sins are forgiven." The bag rolls off his back and falls down the hill into the pond.

Anyone who has ever carried a heavy pack knows the sensation.

Drop the pack. Immediately the hiker feels free. A sense of lightness and a sense of being able to spring forward with new life comes over one. In the Bible, forgiveness does not mean denial of the past. Rather, it comes to mean removal of the effect of the past upon the present. This feeling of freedom from bondage to the past relates both to low moments and to high. Psalm 130 speaks of one crying out or calling. "Deep calls to deep." In that moment, the forgiveness of God becomes clear in the depths.

Similarly, the Psalms of praise – from Psalm 100 on – speak of things that went well but warn of keeping ones eye on God. The psalm writers admit that they, in the midst of all that went well, needed to keep the God who is God as their primary focus—that is as the basic, cosmic perspective. Not to do so is to live in "the sins of the fathers." We can be "bound" by past success as much as past failures. With Adam and Eve, we can think we are like God. The Psalms of Praise help us avoid that mistake. The Psalms force us, in our thanks, to praise God.

There are a number of other Hebrew words that convey the sense of forgiveness as an experience. These may be translated "to cover," "to pardon," and to "wipe away." In each, nothing hides the reality of the sin.

In the Hebrew word "*macha*," for example, the primary meaning is "to stroke" or "to rub over." The sin is still there. The effect of the sin is removed.

## *The Unforgivable Sin*

Mark 3:7 reads as follows: "Truly, I tell you, people will be forgiven for their sins and whatever blasphemies they utter, but whoever blasphemes against the Holy Spirit can never have forgiveness, but is guilty of an eternal sin."

That there could be an "unforgivable sin" goes against the grain for many people. That anything would be unforgivable flies in the face of God's grace.

I had opportunity to see an interesting, unpublished study at the University of California of attitudes toward "unforgivability." The report showed that Protestants have much more difficulty accepting the idea of the "unforgivable" than those who are Jewish. The difficulty theologically is that we must not put limits on God. The difficulty practically is that we must make a difference between the acts and the process.

In discussions about what might be unforgivable, the temptation is to look at a murder, or a rape, or the holocaust, and say, "That was unforgivable." As an emotional response, we can all understand that statement. We all do it. However, all Christian groups make a difference between sins – some are worse than others. Any act can be sinful. It is not the act that cannot be forgiven. *It is the rejection of the very process or dynamic of forgiveness itself that is unforgivable.* People can and do reject the process of forgiveness. People reject the Holy Spirit.

In rejecting the process, people such as dictators do not and will not look at their own need to be forgiven. They will do that which prevents another from experiencing the process of life. As we saw in the experience of Tamar, rape does that. Rape is a form of oppression that denies the process of forgiveness. Rape violates the process of a person's forgiveness of another and of oneself.

Therefore, it is not the act alone that determines whether or not one can forgive but what the act does. Rape denies a life process every bit as much as choking one to death. According to a report in the Korean news, just such denial caused a young woman to jump off the bridge after she was violated. The serial violator denies the use of the process of forgiveness and thus must be pulled out of society. That is the only protection for society. Whether or not that means a sentence should be "life without parole" or execution is a matter for evaluation in each individual case.

Here, the points are:

1) There is such a thing as people totally rejecting the process of healing, the processes of God, and rejecting it now and in any other time after death.

2) There is such a thing as ruining a person's capacity to step into the process of forgiveness – eg. child molestation.

Therefore, at the end of the book of Revelation, *all* sin is thrown into the sea, and the "lake of fire" and then "is no more" (Revelation 20:14-15) In the final New Jerusalem, people do not reject the process, sin disappears, and we find a New Adam.

## Context, Meditation, and Instrument as in Scripture

As we concluded the first chapter, I mentioned the process of forgiveness as involving a context, a mediator, and an instrument. As we look at the Bible, we have now seen developments of these same three parts of the process of forgiveness. In the next chapter we concentrate on that process in detail.

## *Summary*

From this view of the Bible, we see the interplay of human experience both in the Bible and in the studies of science. This interplay is fundamental for a living faith in general and for experiencing the creativity that forgiveness can bring, in particular.

With this background, we now turn specifically to the question of what this understanding of the dynamic of forgiveness means for both an individual of faith and a community of faith. None of this is easy. All of it is possible.

# Chapter Five
## The Interplay of Context, Mediator, and Instrument

### Section I

### Introduction

We have defined the practice of forgiveness as that which releases the power to live creatively. In making that definition, I have identified two dimension of forgiveness: the contextual dimension that must be mediated; the instrumental dimension that is an action in which the context becomes real.

When it comes to places where the word "forgiveness" is not used but the context and instrument free one to be creative, I have identified a correlation between the word "forgiveness" and that power of creativity.

To say that there is a correlation is not to say that forgiveness and the freedom to be creative are synonymous. Forgiveness is also defined as a letting go, of a ceasing to be angry, as a healing. In the examples used in this chapter, the examples are picked because they illustrate the correlation and not because they are a substitute for each other.

## *The Interplay of Context, Mediation, and Instrumental Action*

What then is the specific process of forgiveness that releases the power of creativity? We have established that the brain needs a context in which it can do its work. Yet what really happens? Dr. Matthew Erdelyi, Professor of Psychology at Brooklyn College and Graduate School tells us that Freud himself saw context as "a decisive molder and shifter of perception."[60] (Erdelyi, Matthew Hugh, "The Unconscious, Art, and Psychoanalysis" as in *Psychoanalysis and Contemporary Thought*. International Universities Press, Inc., Madison, CT , 1999)

Musicologists identify the opening lines of a musical score as setting a context. A musicologist at the pre-concert lecture for the San Francisco Symphony identified the context of "different worlds" set by three composers from three different periods of western European history – Mozart, Beethoven, and Ades. The same is true of the opening note of Wagner's Ring Cycle – a note that represents the context of creation.

A threatening context allows for only part of the brain to work – the older part of the brain takes over with defensive actions of "flight or fight."

By contrast, a caring context allows the whole brain to work. The caring dimension of forgiveness allows the whole brain to work in both the offended individual and the one needing forgiveness

To get the point, consider what happens when someone confronts a threat to ones life – when a stranger approaches on a dark street, a wild animal snarls, or confronts.

If that threat materializes and attacks, the flight or fight mechanism of the brain takes over. That attacking context prevents the brain from doing the integration that the process for forgiveness needs. In an attack, there is no space for a "time out" or a creative response to the threat.

Yet, the threat still must be mediated or brought up from our memory field so that, from experience, we know we have a context of danger. A gun, a growl, or a look can provide that mediation. The growl, the posture, or the tilt of the head all mediate the message of the context. That message destroys the process of forgiveness and puts one into a fight or flight mode.

If you or I are the ones attacked, there needs to be some act, some instrument on our part that brings the whole reality into focus. When we run or fight, we not only deal with the attack, we know that we are in danger and in an attack. Questions of forgiveness come later. At the moment, we respond to the attack whether or not that attack is real or imagined. As we respond, we know the depth of the reality in which we find ourselves – the reality of the threat. We may or may not react appropriately. Yet we know that we are in danger. We know we must do whatever we can to survive.

When it comes to a caring context, the role of forgiveness as a process can replace the flight or fight response. I think of a parishioner who said, "That person makes me feel like me." I think of a couple who went to a group therapy session and said, "The thing is, you care."

Why the importance of care? Specifically, care does much more than provide a feeling of security or a freedom to be open, honest, and able to take risks. Care says, "You count where you are and just as you are." Care says, "You are of worth." That is true of a parent holding a child who cries or a Mother Teresa who ministers to a dying man in a gutter.

Any context needs something that communicates that context itself. Be it a healthy and good context or a sick and dangerous context, an individual, a picture, a book, or a ritual need to communicate it. Any or all of our senses may mediate the context of forgiveness and of care. What we see, hear, smell, touch, or taste play a role in that mediation.

What comes through our senses leads to emotional reactions that result in a feeling about what we have seen, heard, tasted, or smelled. Welcoming sights, sounds, tastes, and smells give us the freedom to think, to absorb, and then to decide what to do about the whole mediated context.

We generally do not think of the senses as involved in forgiveness. Yet consider what happens: Someone bumps into us. We feel angry. The person says "Excuse me." Eyes meet and we immediately react: "Is the person sincere, is what happened obviously an accident, is the person in a rush, is the person any one of a number of things?" What we see of body language immediately goes through the eyes to the optic nerve to the key spot in the back of the brain and gets shot to the cerebral cortex in the front of the brain for a decision. The same is true with the smell of alcohol on another's breath.

A group of European researchers has spoken of the "cognitive role" of the "medial frontal cortex" – that part of the brain toward the top and front of our brains that surrounds the mid-brain. (Richard Ridderinkhof et al in *Science*, Vol 306, 2006,4 p. 443).

Research tells us that forgiveness itself has many facets in the brain with a final act of putting all together. This "putting all together" allows us to have an opinion and the opinion becomes a basis for a decision. As noted before, what we see goes to the back of the brain and then shoots to the front of the brain for processing and decision making.

We can say the same thing about hearing. We hear clearly or we do not. We hear a sincere tone or a sarcastic tone or a "drop dead" tone.

What we hear also ultimately gets to that same cognitive part of the brain and becomes part of the decision making process.

Or consider smell—the person who smelled of alcohol. We may smell alcohol on the breath of the person who bumped us. Our initial irritation or anger may lead to a feeling of disgust. If we have a medical background, we may smell something that tells us, "This person is in trouble" or "This person is dangerous."

As for food, the breaking of bread together shows a practice of trust that allows forgiveness to be at work. The shared meal makes real the forgiveness once established.

All this information from the senses becomes part of a complex field -- that creative force or energy that activates the whole brain from the reptilian part through the emotions to the executive part.

Yet one more critical observation about care: *the power to receive care is as important as the power to give it* This observation of the late James Luther Adams of the Harvard Divinity School – and earlier of the Federated Theological Faculty of the University of Chicago – emphasizes the interpersonal nature of the process of forgiveness. There is a field dimension to this dynamic of forgiveness. The matter is not just what goes on in my brain, as we will note in a moment, but what goes on in the brain of the other person in the process of forgiveness. Both the forgiver and the forgiven have a role in the success of the power of forgiveness as a whole.

## *The Cognitive Dimension of Forgiveness*

There are those who speak of the differences between the right and left hemispheres of the brain. The right hemisphere is seen to deal more with the creative, the artistic, or the feeling parts of the brain than the left hemisphere. The left hemisphere is seen as dealing more with the cognitive or thinking parts. Yet those distinctions can become too simplistic.

Certainly there are functions that can be pin pointed, but complex functions involve a "dialogue" of many parts of the brain. When it comes to the complex process of forgiveness, whatever leads to the presence or absence of forgiveness comes from more than just one function in one area of the brain.

More specifically then, what is the actual dynamic of forgiveness in the brain?

We have the work of Tom Farrow on forgiveness specifically.

As reported in the NEUROREPORT, Col 12, No 11 of 8 August, 2001, both empathetic judgments and judgments as to what is forgivable activated the "left superior frontal gyrus, the orbitofrontal gyrus, and the precuneus." (These technical phrases refer to the locations of a ridge in the folds of the brain and before the "V" shaped portion that goes down from that ridge. One is higher – superior- in the cortex and the other forward or frontal)

Those are the technical names for the specific spots where the fMRI registered activity.

What Dr. Farrow emphasizes lifts up the location and activity of decision-making in the brain. In that article, Dr. Farrow defined forgiveness in line with the Oxford Dictionary as the "ceasing to feel angry or resentful towards another."

Please note the word "feel." If one speaks of just an intellectual, unfeeling statement of "All right I forgive you," what do we have?

Frankly, we have nothing. What is done with this cognitive side of the left hemisphere must be at a level that has an effect on the right hemisphere as well.

Just as with the context of an attack, the context of care also requires on our part a response that makes real for the other person and for us that caring context. If we are the one doing the forgiving, the very act confirms for us that we too are forgiven and are free to deal creatively with the person who has offended us. In this sense, the context we provide another serves also as the instrument that demonstrates to us ourselves that we can act as a forgiven people.

Please also note that nothing is said here about what the action must be that makes the forgiveness real to the forgiver or the one forgiven.

It is easy to assume that the action that makes forgiveness real is the action of "reconciliation." Forgiveness may lead to reconciliation, but forgiveness is not reconciliation in and of itself. There is *no automatic* cause and effect relation between forgiveness and reconciliation. In fact, the effect of forgiveness may be the freedom, in a marriage, in a business, even in a church, to have a creative divorce!

It is the freedom to act creatively that is at the heart of the power of forgiveness. A creative divorce allows people to separate without destroying each other. That act is an instrument that makes real the presence of forgiveness. Reconciliation is such an act – but only one example of such an act.

## *Forgiveness and Decision Making*

In an excellent article on creativity in the Scientific American magazine *Mind,* (May 2005 p. 21), a physician and medical writer in Germany identified artistic and other creativity as being primarily a right hemisphere product. The left hemisphere is the more logical and "disciplined" part of the brain. Writes Dr. Urich Kraft: "It is the left hemisphere that conducts this self-evaluation as creative thoughts bubble up from the right." As Ned Herrmann, artist, actor, management trainer and author of *The Creative Brain* (Ned Hermann Group, 1995) notes, "the left brain keeps the right brain in check." Creativity involves the entire brain.

*Forgiveness, then, becomes a decision to evaluate the feelings of the right hemisphere, to let go of feelings of anger and resentfulness, and to let the creative aspect of the left hemisphere move ahead. In that sense, then, forgiveness is a process of the entire brain even as we see that creativity is a process of the entire brain.*

That relation leads to the definition of forgiveness we have used in this book: forgiveness is the cognitive decision to be free from bondage to anything in the past. That freedom allows one to release the creative power of the field of force to deal with the past, the present, and the future.

## *Section II*

## *The Mode of Evaluation*

Given all that process, we now evaluate what happens in an area that involves this dynamic of forgiveness. We pick up the perspectival method and apply it. I use three stories from the Bible–the event of the paralytic healed by Jesus (Mark 2), the event of Job who lost everything and questions God; and the death of Jesus on the cross who also questions God. We then turn to three case studies.

## *The Three Biblical Examples*

As we look at the biblical references, in line with the perspectival method, we are primarily observers. However, within each story, we can speak of different perspectives from which different people speak.

In the story of the paralytic, the story of Job, and the story of Jesus, we have three people who suffer. The one has loss of health, the second lost his children in death and has poor health, and the third is dying a painful execution.

In the story of the paralytic (Mark 2) as in the story of Adam and Eve, the issue is not the "how" of the miracle but the process of the healing.

In this event, Jesus is in an upper room. The place was too crowded. People could not get to him. Given the construction of homes in those days, the second floor room served as the gathering room. Because of the crowd, the four friends carried the paralyzed man to the roof. There they could pull aside the palm leaves and lower the man in front of Jesus.

Some people speak of the four men as representing the context provided by the church. The four men basically helped with the process by putting the sick man in the presence of a person who mediated the context of care – viz. Jesus.

As the one who mediated the context, Jesus spoke to the man not of his legs but of forgiveness. The crowd questioned his right to forgive – only God could do that.

Jesus replied, "Which is it easier to do, to say 'You are forgiven' or to say 'Take up your bed and walk'?" The man walked. *That walk became the instrumental action that made the forgiveness real to him and to everyone else.*

In this example, we then have a process that begins with a contextual dimension—the context mediated by the four who carried the ill man and the context of Jesus before whom they placed the man. In this event, we then have *the instrumentation of action* that made the forgiveness real—the man's walk.

In the case of Job, we have a man for whom God becomes so real that he has a tremendous argument with God. In that argument, Job proclaims his innocence.

In a powerful rebuttal, God is pictured as saying, in effect, "You Job are not God."

We should not look at this instance as a model for counseling. We must look at it for what the author is trying to get across. The purpose of the speech by God is to establish who the Creator is and who is not. The purpose of the story is to give a shock treatment, as it were, of the cosmic context in which we live and the lives that are all about us.

We can consider God as the facilitator, Job as the one facilitated, and us as the observers. Those three perspectives give us an appropriate basis for evaluating this event.

Archibald MacLeish in his play *J.B.* presented Job's wife, Job's friends, and "old women by the wall" as the observers – observers who basically did not "get it." As in most counseling situations, the problem was not Job's innocence or lack of it; the problem was the balance between the forces for healing and creativity on one hand and the life of Job as a human being on the other.

What happened?

From the standpoint of God the facilitator, his letting Job go through this misery in life has finally worked. The speech mediated the creator in a way that Job could get the point and then, himself, become a new person – a new creator in the image of God who knew that he was not God.

From the perspective of Job as the one facilitated, he was the one who got healed in the midst of his sufferings and who therefore found himself, and God, and the fullness of life. The fact that he recovers from bankruptcy is not the healing but must be seen as the result of his recovery.

From the perspective of any of us who are observers, this is a story that teaches us much but also raises questions for us.

As an observer, I learn much about suffering. As a pastoral theologian, I see in this story lessons about the difference between pain and suffering. I also see suffering as having a positive as well as a negative side because I see suffering as a choice. Pain itself is not a choice; it is a condition.

Something very similar we see in the story of Jesus on the cross.

As a matter of fact, the victory in this story comes on the cross – the resurrection, as with Job's recovery of his business and a new family, is but the logical outcome of the victory on the cross. (That is why we call "Good Friday" good.)

So it is that in Jesus we have a good man betrayed, sentenced, and crucified. On the cross, he is heard as saying, "Forgive them."

*This statement turns the cross into the context of forgiveness that is mediated through the very way in which Jesus deals with death and dying.*

In every account of the death, Jesus cries out with some form of protest – he is quoted as saying "My God, why have you forsaken me" or as saying "I thirst." Both statements express total loss.

These statements were heard in different ways. Some misunderstood and thought he called for Elijah. Some thought it evidence that Jesus was a good man. Some thought, "Surely, this is the son of God."

Whatever the words meant, the cry of agony broke through to people in a way that mediated a sense of something greater and more wonderful than any had realized. The context mediated by this dying man indicates that he never lost the integrity of who he was.

Again, we can look at this story from three perspectives.

As the one who went through the experience, students of the Bible often speak of "the work of Christ." Some reduce that work to one who was a revolutionary, others to a person fiercely obedient to what he felt called to be, and still others as a person so at one with God that he incarnated (embodied) the oneness with God or the forgiveness of God. Although I identify with the latter two more than the revolutionary stance, the focus here is on the reality and necessity of someone who mediates that context so that we see it. We know that we operate in it. When we do see Jesus in that perspective, we see him as the "one pushed" to use Feldman's word or the one "facilitated" to use my word. We can also look at the crucifixion from the perspective of those who brought it about. The facilitators can be seen as the Roman soldiers, the crowd that paid no attention, or, as Bach does in the St. Matthew Passion, as any of us.

...And we can see the crucifixion from the perspective of the observer – which is what happens when the Bible is read as literature.

## *Section III*

## *Three "Modern" Stories*

With these biblical models in mind, let us now look at three contemporary examples. I had a role in each example. In each example, by way of demonstration, I will pick one perspective from which to look at the experience. I will present these events in the third person.

At the time of the assassination of President Kennedy the role of any priest, pastor, or Rabbi came to be one of facilitating the healing process of grief. In the Columbine shootings, a group of colleagues became observers who heard the story from members of the community who were involved. In the story of the shooting of the Amish children, we will use the perspective of those who, intimately involved in faith groups, felt involved with the faith group that was attacked.

# *The Assassination of John F. Kennedy.*

As just said, my basic perspective of a report on the experience of that assassination came as one who was in Feldman's word an *agent* or in my word a *facilitator*.

As the day developed, the pastor of the Westminster Presbyterian Church in Bloomfield, New Jersey, had two communities to serve. One was the parish of the church itself. The other was the high school student body to whom he was asked to speak at a special assembly. He therefore served two wounded and grieving communities.

News of the assassination had come in blunt words: "The President has been shot. President John Fitzgerald Kennedy is dead."

The words stunned all, but two specific moods emerged—that of grief and that of guilt.

Any death cuts through the nonessential. At a death, people realize how much they have focused on the unimportant. They may remember things done they wish they had not done, and in the words of one prayer book they feel, "There is no health in us."

In such a moment, a child may remember little things such as "did I tell Grandpa how much I liked the toy he gave me?" A husband whose wife has just died may ask, "Did I tell her that I loved her before she died?" To the person of faith, regardless of his or her espoused belief, a Gospel song may have new meaning – such as "Amazing Grace" that one should die for "a wretch like me."

Regardless of party politics, the Kennedy death brought feelings of remorse, embarrassment, guilt, or shame. These feelings had to be addressed. For freedom to handle the anger and the sense of loss, the congregation needed a process to get beyond the initial emotions. All needed to feel forgiven.

Partly people needed a context of care in order to face the particular guilt that confronted them. That guilt and the deeper sense of shame were different for different people. For many, the guilt centered on the jokes some made about the President.

In a popular comedy routine of the day, a comedian poked fun at the President. The routine said that the President dreamt about Abraham Lincoln. In the dream, President Kennedy asked Lincoln what he would do in some particularly difficult situation. According to the comedian, in the dream Lincoln replied, "Well, I went to the theater."

The "joke" had been told years earlier by many Republicans who abhorred Franklin Delano Roosevelt. The story brought a laugh then, and the joke brought a laugh again when applied to President Kennedy. The comedy routine sold many records. The moment of the assassination, sales ended, and the comedian went into eclipse.

That was but one of the many emotional responses.

Although both at the church and at the school the pastor became an agent of change, the situation at the two places proved totally different.

The constant in both situations is that the facilitator had to set the context for the moment at hand. In each instance, the task was to bring people from their different worlds with their different contexts into the context that the pastor mediated. The dynamics of the church congregation and of the high school audience required different means for dealing with the same experience, but the task was the same.

In the context of the church, the Sunday after November 22$^{nd}$ was "Thanksgiving Sunday." All in the pastoral role had to rethink their sermons. The pastor at Westminster began, "If this were a day of national tragedy, would we still give thanks?"

Amongst the many emotions came the questions –

"Did we do enough?"

"Had I been unfair?"

"Why did this have to happen?"

"Where was God?"

Two other facts confronted all pastors:

First, all had to face larger-than-usual congregations on that Sunday. Attendance at church always increases after a national tragedy such as D-day, the Palm Sunday after Martin Luther King's death, the blow up of the space ship Columbia, or the devastation of 9/11.

Second, many in the congregations were Republican As had been the case with Republicans when Franklin Roosevelt died, those of the party and persuasion different from the President would have a special mixture of emotions and feelings.

The pastor's task became one of mediating God's love to people who were asking serious questions about themselves.

In dealing with two groups of the church and the school, pastors also had to ask the question, "Who is the patient?" When speaking to an audience, the audience is itself as much the counselee as any individual. On this occasion, the pastor had the community of the church and the community of the school student body. The emotions and dynamics of each community became as important as the emotions and dynamics of the individual.

In the dynamics of the two audiences, one could sense a field of force in the groups as a whole and in the dynamics of the sanctuary or the school auditorium. In that situation, *the speaker discovered that he had a role in embodying that context.*

The task then of the speaker, from the perspective of the agent of change, lay in bringing both groups and the individuals in both groups to the point of freedom to move on creatively with their own lives.

The task was neither to deal with grief alone nor to be inspirational. What we have learned about empathy and the brain tells us at least four aspects of the role of the "agent":

1) Since the pastor shared the feelings of the two communities,

the first task was to lift that common feeling to conscious awareness. Only then could all look at it, recognize the shared feelings, and deal with them.

2) The pastors themselves needed to experience God's love and care sufficiently that they could mediate that care to the different communities. The task was one of giving such witness through words and body language that the activity in the speaker's brain could and would be replicated in the brain of each person in the two different communities.

   a. Given that one place was a church and the other a school, the method could not be the same, but the task was the same.

3) The matter of experiencing this forgiveness and communicating it to others was *a choice*.

   a. That truth meant finding time for the speaker to work through those feelings.

   b. The pastor needed to act in such a way as to give all "permission" to have their own feelings and work on them. People also needed encouragement to move on to the next steps in life. In this dynamic, it is not just what the speaker says but who the speaker allows him or her self to be that makes the difference.

4) For the pastor himself, the very act of being the agent of change and having the freedom to move on with his ministry proved healing. Therefore, in line with the process of forgiveness, the context the speaker offers to others also becomes his or her instrument of experiencing the reality of the cosmic context of forgiveness. In such a situation, a speaker can then give guidance as to what others may do in helping work through their feelings. In doing so, the forgiveness as freedom to act

creatively becomes real and one can move on with life.

In concluding this brief description of what was a process of several days, I should mention the totally different contexts of the two organizations.

*In the church*, a pastor is the agent in charge. The community looks to the pastor the leader – the caregiver as it were. Under that leadership, the preparation began for the service of worship. The leadership of the church developed a liturgy. Others such as the choir and the sexton all had different roles. In the process, not just the pastor but the group as a whole became the context for everyone. As in baseball the pitcher gets credit for the win or loss of a game, so in the church, that pastor gets the praise or the blame for the success of a time of worship. Yet, in the church as in the baseball team, the corporate body itself became the agent of change. Whereas the pastor began as the facilitator, the congregation not only provided the forgiving context, *the congregation became* the forgiving context.

*In the school,* the pastor was not in charge and there was not the same corporate structure as in the church.

At the school, the Principle was in charge and introduced the speaker who was a pastor – but not pastor to the school.

In the Bloomfield High School, the Superintendent of schools and other officials moved back and forth at the rear of the hall. Rather than the beautiful sanctuary to surround the speaker, the audience saw only a stark stage with a black backdrop and a U.S. flag in the corner. Here, the speaker had to become the leader, establish relationships with the audience, and thus create the context for the audience. Here, however, the audience did not become the agent of change in the way the church group did. There was not the sense of personal relationships that had developed over the years in the church congregation.

*Rev. James Emerson*

## *Columbine Revisited*

In the tragedy of the shootings at Columbine, the role of most of us was the role of an *observer*. Some of us who gathered at Columbine to talk about trauma found ourselves as observers in a special way. We were part of a seminar conducted by workers and survivors of those shootings.

The shootings at the Columbine school in Lakewood, Colorado caught the emotions of people all over the North American continent and in many parts of the world. Several years after the shootings, some forty of us who are professionals in the pastoral care field met with a two panels of people involved.

One panel was made up of parents – one whose son was injured, one whose daughter was murdered, and one who survived without physical wounds.

The other panel was made up of professionals – the school principle, a police chief, a social worker, a teacher, and a pastor. That these people might need to deal with the issue of forgiving others, any can understand. Given my point of needing to forgive ourselves, where does that fit here? The need for personal forgiveness came from many directions:

- "Survivor guilt" that says, "how come they got killed or injured and I survived?"
- Shame from a feeling of having been unprepared to deal with such a shooting.
- Shame for realizing that help was needed and one either did not offer it or did not know how to offer it.
- Guilt that goes with grief that reminds one of ways in which he or she had not fulfilled responsibilities for others.

114

Actually, when a group after a trauma is asked what a tragedy makes them feel, the number of responses often runs out of blackboard space. In addition to these personal feelings, there was also a group sense of "if only" that kept appearing in different ways. "If only I had sensed the tell tale signs," "if only I had been there," "if only she had kept quiet" and similar thoughts came again and again in the discussion.

The result of these presentations was manifold. Each person told of the feelings that he or she had had in the past and had then. The mother of the girl who was shot said, "Call it what it was; my daughter was murdered. I get sick and tired of people trying to give explanations or give what happened a name that is less than what it really was."

This call for precision in description was critical not only for her but for all the participants.

The school principle spoke of hearing the shots but not accepting the reality of the situation until he opened the door. There, he could see the students running and the boys with the guns coming. "It" was happening. As the principle saw the gunmen advance down the hall, a classroom door on his left opened. He slammed the door shut to face the guns himself. With that, a teacher came down a staircase from the side – a teacher who was helping and rescuing students. The student gunmen saw the teacher and killed him instead of the principle.

The mother of an injured son who had spent months in rehab after the shooting told of her son's trauma and permanent injuries. She went on to say that that son had gone on to the completion of his studies, to marriage, and to a responsible place in life.

Note that in each instance we have an example of the perspectival method – each member of the panel spoke from definite and clear perspectives as agents. Each also spoke from the perspective of one emotionally traumatized. The rest of us in our discussion were the observers.

The panel members probably could not have spoken as they did had we been present in the early weeks of the shootings. Now, thanks to the passage of time, they could. The result was development of the kind of precision spoken of by Professor Feldman and positive results as to the "truth" with which each had to deal.

For each of us there, the developing empathy meant that each of us also identified with the feelings and issues of one or another of those who spoke. There were messages given by each and points that they wanted to have clear. For each of us as a caregiver or a parent or a school leader, however, the situation meant that we had to deal not only with the emotions and questions we had when we arrived at the meeting, but we had to deal with the feelings that developed in the meeting.

## *The Amish School Children*

Those of us who have lived part or more of our lives in Pennsylvania or Ohio have more than a passing acquaintance with people who are Amish.

We have driven past their horse drawn buggies on the road. We have seen their clean and productive farms. Some of us have had moments of worship with them and times of fellowship and study.

The news broke of a man named Roberts who went to a small, Amish schoolhouse and killed innocent youngsters. The fact that these were Amish children had special impact on some of us.

How was this situation any different from listening to the folks at Columbine?

Those in any faith community feel an affinity with those or similar faith communities. Further, for some of us, there is an identification that comes from our having friends and colleagues who are part of an Amish community.

Along with the tragedy and the shock of what had happened, four things became immediately clear – the closeness of the cosmic sense of God's love to each individual and to the community; the depth of the community ties that included the sinner as well as the sinned against; the use of space and time to get hold of emotions and experience; and the immediate action to bring healing and strength to others.

Who could imagine a group of people going to the families and friends of the murderer as quickly as to the families and friends of the children who had died? What was operative for those who DID go to the families of both the children and the one who pulled the trigger?

At the outset, in the midst of all that happened, in the Amish we have a people with a tremendous sense of being in the context of the cosmic – in the context of the creator of the universe as seen in Job and in Jesus on the cross.

This sense is reinforced again and again by their closeness to the soil, their avoidance of that which interferes with a sense of being one with creation, and not just a view but a feeling of the mediation of Jesus Christ.

This feeling of being part of the cosmic is reflected again by being part of a community that is not as great as the cosmos but is greater than any one person. The experience of John Donne in his poem "For whom the bell tolls" gets fulfilled in their feeling a part of each other. No one is an "isle unto himself."

This reality came alive for them in an action which served as an instrument of realizing that all were in the context of a cosmic forgiveness. To get that realization, forgiveness became a discipline in itself that they all followed.

In their experience, all we have said about the brain, the field of empathy and the process of forgiveness came alive. It is not that the brain studies tell something that they did not know. It is that the brain studies deepen everyone's understanding of empathy and what it is to have neurons firing in one person's brain also firing in the brain of another.

Likewise, Tom Farrow's confirmation that in the activity of the brain, forgiveness is a choice has an example in the Amish group.

So deep is the sense of forgiveness amongst the Amish that they literally showed an extraordinary freedom to meet, to bind up wounds, and to minister to each other. That ministry included ministry to the Roberts' family (the family of the gunman). It was that very ministering to each other that brought the healing not only to those who suffered the loss, but to the health of the whole community itself.

## *Observations*

From the standpoint of discussing the dynamic of forgiveness, I will not make any attempt to do an in depth evaluation of any of these three events.

However, I invite the reader to think first of his or her ways of dealing with these events. If you were not alive at the time, imagine how you would feel if any of the presidents you have known were assassinated, of how you would feel if the school shooting had been in your high school or the one nearest where you have lived, or indeed in your own faith community. Murder is a terrible act that hits more than the individuals involved. We all become victims.

## *Notes in Common*

1) Note at the outset the degree to which the instrumental actions became operative.

   a. The purpose in writing the above was to share a sense of how others can find bases for understanding crisis events in which forgiveness and healing are dimensions.

b.  The fact is that in writing these reflections as one who had his own emotions, feelings, and senses of inadequacy, the experience has given me a sense of closure and, once again, of the context of forgiveness. When done in the context of a community of faith, this writing would be called a "confession." The writing of the above statements is one demonstration of an instrument that helps make forgiveness real to me as the writer.

2)  A common note shows up in the need for a context within which to deal with the tragedies. Each tragedy needed a mediator that embodied the context. In each tragedy all needed an instrument of action that made the forgiveness real to the one who carried out the action

3)  Each event had and needed an opportunity for anger and the time to understand and deal with that anger.

4)  Note the need for "closure" in each community.

## *Note of Difference*

1)  Note the different types of context for those in Columbine, in the Amish community, and in Bloomfield.

    a.  As mentioned in the reports themselves, the context for intervention in Bloomfield, New Jersey, constantly changed from church to school and back to the church.

    b.  This change of context in Bloomfield meant that the speaker helped define the context whereas in Columbine and with the Amish, the community remained pretty much the context.

2)  The clearest difference was the sense of the "body" or the

community of the Amish as opposed to the situation with the two school shootings in which all—victims and families—were part of separate communities that became a new community simply because of the killing.

3) Another difference lay in the handling of anger. All the groups had the opportunity and reason for anger, but the management of anger was varied.

   a. Anger can come from many sources. It may be anger of betrayal, anger over loss, anger over feelings brought newly to light by the new crime.

   b. These differences in anger require different interventions. It is important for caregivers to help individuals sense the different areas and deal with them.

Finally, I would emphasize again the clear sense of forgiveness in the forgiveness of God–that is, in the cosmic dimension that provided the under girding for the Amish community.

## *The Role of Forgiveness.*

Given the above, what then do we say about forgiveness?

From the brain studies, we observe that we have here not only a process but a process that allows us to move on in life. Creativity can replace destruction. Those researchers are right who hold that forgiveness is a means of dealing with issues that separate people.

In each of the above, nothing could change the past nor bring back the dead. We must, therefore, find a means of letting go of the past in such a way as to move forward to the future.

The Amish understood this latter expectation of forgiveness.

Yet they too had to deal with the question of how to get closure. Some opted for tearing down the schoolhouse. Others wanted to keep it. Although the decision was finally to tear down the school, which then symbolized starting off with a new beginning, the task was to decide what in fact made real the context of love and forgiveness.

As human beings, we all are part of communities. We all need to learn how to live in the community dynamic as well as the individual dynamic of our private lives.

## *Conclusion*

In looking back over these experiences from the Bible and from life events in which I had some share, I am more and more impressed with the reality of the contextual, the need for what mediates the contextual, and instrumental-action aspects of forgiveness. These aspects involve the whole brain.

I am also impressed with the degree to which an act that prevents the whole of the process becomes the unforgivable sin. The discipline of forgiveness is necessary for the power of creativity to be unleashed. The neurons of our brains need the practice of that discipline. The health of the individual and the health of the society require that discipline.

Sometimes a physical failure will make it impossible for the whole brain to sustain the process of forgiveness – primarily a brain injury or atrophy of the nervous system.

When these mechanical features break down, western law recognizes the impairment in deciding guilt or innocence. When, however, there is an attack on the process of forgiveness itself, then the power cannot be released and we have that for which there is no pardon.

Our task, then, is to find those activities which prepare us for the process of forgiveness and allow the process to work. In part III, we will look at how the church, as one institution, tried to develop those processes through the centuries. We then will turn again to current case studies.

# Suggested Exercises in Identifying the Dynamic of Forgiveness

The Context
1) Write out a situation in which you spoke with one person.
2) What was the physical context of the setting?
3) What context did the other person provide for you?
4) Look at a meeting you conducted and ask the same questions.
5) Go back to the same situations and ask:
    1) What or who mediated that for you?
        a. Consider the history of your faith community and ask the prior two questions again. Who mediated a context for you?
        b. How were you mediator to them?
        c. What helped you let go?

The Instrument
1) In each of the above situations, what did the other do that served as an instrument to make the context real?
2) In each of the above situations, what did you do that allowed the context to come alive for you?

The History
2) In your family history, can you think of times in which actions (instruments) were imposed on you?
3) In those situations, what could have been done so that the context of forgiveness would have come alive?

# Part Three
## The Practice

### The Practice in History and the Practice Today.

What does all this information mean for everyday living? What is the *practice* of forgiveness that releases the power for creative living?

First take a look at history. How true it is that "those who ignore history are doomed to repeat it." What can we learn from history?

Next, take a look at case studies. . . .

In both the historical dimension and the current, the critical question is this: *how real to an individual or a group is the presence of God--the cosmic "field of force"*? To "feel" that the heart of the universe gives us a context of forgiveness and love is the basic message of scripture and the experience of realized forgiveness.

The dynamic of forgiveness is about that sense of a forgiving context made real in practice. Faith is about how that context is mediated to us. Morality is about how that mediated context comes real to us and to others by virtue of some instrument of action. That holds true in our personal lives and in the politics of the world.

Let us remember that we speak of a process. We speak of a process that allows for such freedom from bondage to the past – be that past good or bad -- that we find an inner wholeness as we let go of the past and move to creative action in the future.

# Chapter Six
## The Church and the Instrument of Forgiveness

### Introduction

In my book of forty years ago, I traced the history of the Jewish and Christian communities of faith in their search for a workable practice of forgiveness. In reading all of the books from Genesis to Malachi, we can see event after event as a correction of the context or the instrument that makes the context real.

Often the instrument of following laws that helped make God's presence real became more important than the than the context of God's love. We see that danger corrected when Jesus said, the "Sabbath was made for humankind not humankind for the Sabbath" (Mark 2:27). The observance of the Sabbath was to be a time of reminding one of the real God. The practice was not to take the place of God.

We see the nature of God violated when the love and judgment of God get reduced to rules and regulations that are less than God. We see that in the prophet Amos who spoke of God "hating our festivals" and wanting justice to roll down like waters of righteousness (which means "right relations" with God) (Amos 5: 21 ff.). We see the same concern in Jesus and the interpretations of Paul.

## *The Rhythm of History*

There is a rhythm to this process of correction throughout history. The philosopher Hegel spoke of the rhythm as moving from thesis to antithesis to a new synthesis. The synthesis becomes a new thesis and the rhythm repeats itself. We see the rhythm in a comment I once saw in a compendium of Luther's writings in which he said that a liturgy for worship should be rewritten every two years. We see that again in a statement I heard made by the theologian Karl Barth that every generation needed to restate the creed in its own culture and its own language.

Something similar is taking place on college campuses today. From pastors to students in college and universities, we learn that it no longer is out of place to talk about religious issues. Only students often reject the word "religion." The association of religion with religious wars of today makes the word repellent. Institutional religion gets damned as too narrow.

Instead, students more and more speak of "spirituality." These college students want to begin with a cosmic context that transcends them, and they also want an opportunity to make that context real with various approaches to prayer, meditation, and worship. Because the institutional approach feels too restrictive in style and substance, these students reject the institutional approach.

Unfortunately, that approach fails to remember there has to be some "instrumentation" of the spiritual reality. The new spiritually based communities of faith themselves become a form of institution. The problem does not lie in the developing of an organization. The problem lies in the tyranny of the organization as expressed in a street gang, a high school or college clique, an organized faith group or church that says all others are wrong and only they are right. Once a group makes a particular practice absolute, be it a liberal or a conservative group, the practice gets in the way of the forgiving context rather than making it real.

Jesus combined the context and instrument in proper balance when he talked with a Samaritan woman at the well (John 4). On the one hand, he spoke of God as a Spirit. On the other hand, he spoke both of worship (an instrumental action), and sharing the news with other people (another form of instrumental action).

Several places in the history of the Christian communities of faith and worship indicate the struggle for the proper balance. I pick the early church, the Celtic Penitentials, the Benedictine Rule, and the Reformation.

## *The Search in the Early Church*

In the first five centuries different communities of faith formed around the way in which God became real to them in the person of Jesus Christ.

At one point, the context of forgiveness was seen as mediated by the community of faith itself. We see that partly in the book of Acts and further in the writings of people such as Tertullian.

A process ultimately developed in which a person made his or her confession in the presence of the group. Some communities had a person move to the outer circle of the group as a form of atoning for a given sin. As a person moved forward in the group, that move toward the center gave one a sense of being more and more forgiven.

In time such a process became unworkable as need for confidentiality developed. That need lead then to an emphasis on personal prayer. The history of the development of a hermit religion was a swing in the opposite direction. People would go to these hermits to benefit from what those men or women developed in private.

St. Anthony is traditionally described as the first of the hermit saints. Whether or not he was the first, he certainly represents the first of those Christians who would go out into the wilderness to live alone and develop the spiritual dimension of their lives. Augustine in the West and Athanasius in the East paid particular attention to the life and model of Anthony.

Yet, as the individual in prayer became the antithesis of the group in prayer, ultimately a synthesis developed of relating the two in the experience of the group. Some of these groups developed in the East (generally the area around Turkey) under the influence of people called the "Cappadocian Divines."

## *The Benedictine Rule*

In the West, we have the noted work of Benedict (c480—c570 A. D.). The Benedictine movement brought together both the private and the community aspects of the process of worship and forgiveness. His approach to the power for creativity carries down in different religious groups even to this day.

Amongst those in the Order of Benedictines, *The Benedictine Rule is* read almost as much as the Bible. Many, including John Calvin, appear to have been influenced by "the Rule." Many of us in non-Roman Catholic traditions also take it seriously.

*The Rule* is an excellent book on both administrative and devotional practice. The Fifth Chapter of the rule speaks of the administrative role of the Abbot. The chapter speaks of that role in a way that has implications of the force field of the Spirit. The role relates to the treatment of new members. The fifth chapter states that the Abbot is to pay strict attention to even the most recent of the novitiates. The Spirit will speak through the person who is the newest.

Again from the standpoint of what we have been saying about a spiritual "field of force," the arrival of any new person in a community changes the dynamic of that community. The recognition of the new person gives attention to the reality of the field of force. The field changes with the addition of each novitiate.

In the fifth and sixth centuries, Rome fell but the church survived. Gregory the Great, the Pope under whom that survival came, was Benedictine. His balance of context and instrument in the community of faith stood him well.

In one instance, Gregory wrote a young priest. He spoke of being "upon a sea of troubles and almost sunk." The writing of that "confession" itself could have been an instrument that made real his forgiveness and gave Gregory new freedom for the task at hand.

## *The Celtic Penitential*

Another significant development in the history of the church comes from the development of the Celtic Penitential. In their development we see dissatisfaction with the community of the parish church in making forgiveness real. We see an individualistic approach as an individual would go to a particular priest. We then see the whole approach becoming part of the parish community.

Our authority for what happened is the late John McNeil, then of Union Theological Seminary in New York[61] Dr. McNeil focused on the early church and particularly on the Celtic penitential practices in the sixth and seventh centuries. What I present here is not a summary of his work but a simplified picture of the pattern of reformation as we come to look at the practices relevant for today.

131

In some ways what we reported amongst college students of today was anticipated amongst the people of the British Isles of the early centuries. The institutional church simply did not seem able to communicate the experience of forgiveness in such a way that people experienced the power to move on creatively in their lives. However, there were groups formed that developed an effective process of instrumentation.

The Celts of that day in Ireland and Scotland developed a process of confession. An individual would go to a priest, confess, and be given a prescription of what he or she may do. When the person went out to do those things, he or she felt that the forgiveness had become real.

The process and practice of these penitential priests proved inventive and helpful. There was no sense in which the actions were a way of "paying for the sin." Rather, the suggested actions were a way of correcting the behavior. If a person gossiped, the penitential act often would be silence for a required period of time. If a person committed adultery, that individual would be required a period of abstinence. The process was called "a system of contraries."

We may smile at such simplicity. Yet awareness of Hibbs law about dominant neurons gives some basis for a practice that may indeed strengthen other neurons.

So popular did this approach of private confessors become that parish leaders felt the competition. As a result, they brought the confessional into the church and made it part of the parish life.

That move provided a synthesis of the institutional parish and the new practice.

However, as often happens, the synthesis became misused   The action of penance slowly became a means of paying to get into heaven rather than an instrument for making forgiveness real.

## *The Reformation and the Instrumentation of Forgiveness*

In the course of history, something happened with regard to the misuse of the instrument of penance. The experience of penance became the end in and of itself. It became the substitute for God. Its role in the dynamic or the process of forgiveness became the whole thing – and thus failed.

The best known example is that of a monk named Tetzel.

Tetzel sold indulgences which, supposedly, helped get one into heaven. The money went to help with the cost of building St. Peter's basilica. As a result, what had begun as a means of making forgiveness real became a fund-raising device.

Along came people like Martin Luther who found that the practice of penance no longer made forgiveness real for him and became an end in itself. True, different people had different motives for opposing the Pope. Yet legitimately, there were those for whom the misuse of penance flew against everything we now know about the brain and ourselves – namely, we are not static as individuals but individuals in process. We are defined by the reality of process. That process requires a contextual dimension of forgiveness and an instrumental – not just the instrumental.

The inevitable result in the days of the Reformation as in our day was to argue and then fight over what the Reformers came to call the "means of grace" – which I identify as the instruments that brought alive to us the reality of the process of forgiveness.

As time has gone on, Protestants too have made the same mistake.

Some have identified practices other than penance as an end instead of a means to an end. Emphasis on one form of baptism, on speaking in tongues, on the use of certain phrases, and on certain styles of worship have sometimes been used as tests of faith rather than seen as instruments to help faith come alive.

By contrast, historically one thinks of St. Teresa of Lisieux. As a young woman, Teresa did not stay with an institutional congregation but went to a convent. As she became established in that convent, the day came when a novice asked her how to reconcile two writings: the writings from Ecclesiasticus 14:15 that spoke of the "merit of his works" with Paul's statement in Romans that we are "justified freely by grace" (Romans 3:24). Teresa replied that the sacrifice nourishes our faith. "Faith feeds on sacrifice" are her exact words. Teresa added that our personal sacrifice is *not* what "saves us." (From a devotional booklet, *Just for Today, Writings of St. Teresa of Lisieux with selections from the Imitation of Christ,* compiled by A Benedictine of Stanbrook, Worcester, Burns and Oates, Belgium, 1943, 1963 edition, p, 231)

Therefore in words different from what we now use in the light of the dynamic of forgiveness, Teresa made clear that the forgiveness does not come because of the works. The works simply help bring the forgiveness into our awareness.

A major shift on the part of the Reformation to allow for the proper use of the balance between context and instrument is the concept of the priesthood of all believers. That concept seeks to put ordained and non-ordained on an equal footing before God. More than that, in the serving of the sacrament, any individual may at one moment serve another as a priest and then receive the sacrament from that "other" as a communicant. In this development, we have another example of the synthesis, the rhythm in which changes were made to keep the proper balance between context and instrument.

In this way the process of serving and receiving the Eucharist (the sacrament) demonstrated the whole aspect of the interplay between the context of God's care and the instrument that can make that care real – namely the act that emphasizes "the priesthood of all believers" itself.

At the time of the Reformation, the process for receiving the sacrament was for people to go forward in a sanctuary and receive the sacrament at the altar and at the hands of the priest. During the Reformation, particularly in Zurich, the clergy changed the practice. There the clergy went out into the congregation.

In Holland, a process developed which is a synthesis of the members of the church going forward and the clergy going to the people.

For example, at the New Church in Amsterdam, known as the Neuekirch, a long table goes across the front of the church. At the appointed time, members of the congregation go forward and sit around that table. The officiating pastor conducts the liturgy. The elements are passed from him to the person on the right and the left. Each person passes the elements of the bread and the wine the length of the table. Reflective of the priesthood of all believers, people serve each other. When all have been served around the table, they return to their seats and others go forward.

The act of offering the bread and the wine (or grape juice or water as in some traditions) became the instrument that made the experience of having been forgiven real to the one who offered it. The very act of offering might be seen as an act of practicing the priesthood of the believer who is offering the sacrament. To those who understand it, that very act can be powerfully meaningful.

The act of offering the elements of the bread and wine did for the individual worshipper what "penance," properly understood, did for people. The act of the offering became the context and was the instrument for the one offering. In that practice, the dual dynamic, the yin and the yang, the receiving and the giving were always there.

For some faith groups, the practices that develop are different from what I have just described. For some, such as the Society of Friends, there is no sacrament at all. Yet every group finds something that becomes the instrument that makes real the context of forgiveness.

In the Society of Friends, for example, the very expression of a thought inspired by the Holy Spirit is an instrument that makes what was said real. We understand what we have said better after we have said it than before we have said it. An act or instrument that makes the dimension of forgiveness real in the Friends meeting comes at the end. There, each person turns to those on each side and exchanges a warm handshake.

Thus the dynamic process identified in the psychological studies and now seen in brain studies comes alive in different ways among different faith groups.

## *Penance or Renewal*

Where it seems to me most Protestant groups fail today lies in not recognizing the original intent of the penitential act. Luther and Calvin ruled out the wrong use of penance as a sacrament and as a means of salvation. However, neither of them ruled out the expectation of certain behavior that would logically – or psychologically – grow out of the contexts of love and forgiveness.

Vatican II specifically addressed the concern of the misuse of the act of penance. In the United States, a Catholic Conference pulled the thoughts together in a study manual in 1975.[62] The introduction to the study paper specifically speaks of the role of penance "in the context of a celebration of the word of God."

Yet, a question remains: The word "penance" itself relates to thought of punishment as in the "penal" system of prisons If it is correct that one role of the instrument is that of making one free to move on in a creative way, words such as "renewal" or "restoration" or even redemption should replace the word "penance." The latter word too easily carries the thought of the means of renewal as some form of punishment. On the contrary, the act of renewal in and of itself assumes the recovered wholeness and speaks of the freedom to move on with life.

The study edition of penance regards the act as something to be adapted by each diocese to the "needs of their own regions." That is an improvement but does not speak of the positive awareness of forgiveness reflected in the word "renewal."

## *Difference between Calvin and Luther*

In this whole matter of historical development during the period of the Reformation, we find a difference between Calvin and Luther. (This subject I developed in *The Dynamics of Forgiveness, pp. 145-51*). To make and yet oversimplify the difference: Luther felt that teaching began with teaching the law – the Ten Commandments. In this way, the people would get a sense of how they fall short and of their need to repent and be forgiven. Luther in his catechetical classes then moved from teaching the law to teaching the grace of God who forgives. From that he then moved on to the power for a creative conversation with God which is the act of prayer.

Calvin saw the process differently. Calvin felt that one first had to know the grace of God, and sense it, before the Ten Commandments could help us see the nature of sinful acts. Therefore, Calvin began with what earlier I have called "the cosmic dimension of a perspective." Calvin began with the grace of God, then went to the Ten Commandments which made one aware of our having come short of the high standard, and then spoke of the act of prayer that became both a dialogue with

God and an instrument that lifted up our sense of God's forgiveness of us.

Although my Lutheran friends might well disagree, I feel that the progression of context first and then the instrumental act that makes the forgiveness real is what in fact happens in the Lutheran liturgy.

I recently attended the rededication of a Lutheran church that had been damaged by an earthquake. The obvious attention and money expended on the sanctuary and the affirmation of God in the opening hymn both spoke to the context into which the congregation as a whole and each of us as individuals entered the time of worship. Once that happened, then we all moved to a period of confession.

## *Conclusion*

Throughout history, then, we find the need for a community of faith that mediates the context of God's forgiveness and provides for or guides an action that becomes a means of making that context real.

When the individual or community mediator took itself to be the context and not just the mediator, we had trouble. When the community concretized this or that particular act as the new god, we had trouble. When the balance was maintained, we had a dynamic of forgiveness realized in a moment of time that brought not a mealy mouth approach to life but brought the power of a new creativity in the midst of old problems.

Today, much can be learned about effective ways to develop the instrumentation from different cultures. In the attachments, I reflect on insights from India, from the concept of women as "mothers of the church," from the work of Elaine Pagels in Gnostic writings and from the work of Elsie McGee in the life of a woman reformer named Katharina Schütz Zell.

We turn now to case studies from recent years.

# Chapter Seven
## Models of the Dynamic of Forgiveness

### Introduction

In this chapter, let us look at six areas in which we see the application of the information developed in this book.

### Partners by choice

The first area I suggest is a study by Professor Archie Smith of the United States and his colleague Dr. Ursula Riedel of Germany. The book they wrote together - *Partners by Choice* - underscores an initial point of the research on the brain—forgiveness is a choice. What makes this book a special contribution is that their approach is more sociological than psychological.

From a theological standpoint, everyone agrees that at least God has a choice. In addition, however, the Lutheran Martin Marty identified a hidden discipline in forgiveness – namely, the choice of following the Ten Commandments or not. That means all of us have a choice. Personally, I would see forgiveness itself as the "hidden discipline" of faith, but we all agree on the matter of personal responsibility for our decision.

In our preceding pages, we have pointed out the way in which studies of the brain underscore the matter of choice. Out of England the significant findings from Dr. Farrow identified forgiveness as an act in the thinking, deciding part of the brain. In fact, the whole area of study about forgiveness is moving more and more into the area of the cognition itself.[63] We have the evidence from Dr. Farrow and we have a similar conviction from Drs. Smith and Riedel in *Partners by Choice*.[64]

Forgiveness is a process that allows one part of the brain to address other parts of the brain in a way that empowers us to act creatively. To see how this works, we pick the following areas for examination::

1) An administrative meeting with an administrative council;
2) Three instances of dealing with oppression;
3) A failed instance of marriage counseling;
4) A process of public worship and private prayer,
5) A memorial service of worship.

In each of these, look particularly for the dynamic of forgiveness as the process moves from context to mediation of the context to an instrument of action that creates a new context.

## *Forgiveness in Administration*

A major business went through a change in its Administrative Council. The institution identified itself as a Christian organization open to all. The Board of Directors changed the process for the conduct of the Administrative Council of the staff. The Council meetings had been lead by the COO (Chief Operating Officer). From the time of that meeting on, the Board decreed that the Council would be chaired by the CEO.

Unfortunately, the CEO did not have the best rapport with the Council. Resentment over the change became both personal and political. The move involved not just power but also a symbol of power. The tension made it difficult for the CEO to communicate a message that the others were of worth

In the course of time, various factors conspired. One of those was a social scandal that involved the CEO. Resignation quickly followed.

The Board of Directors chose a former member to serve as the interim CEO – and therefore the chair of the Council.

After he took office, the first major event for the Interim CEO was a staff retreat. Some members of the Council hoped that at that time he would move back to having the COO chair the meetings. However, this interim CEO made clear that he would not change the procedure.

In the comments at the closing session, the new executive addressed the issue of leadership. He asked, "Whom do you regard as the head of this organization?" He concluded "No one in this room!" He went on, "This is a Christian organization and for us, the head is Jesus Christ." "Our task this year, "he said, "is to figure out what that means and how to make that work."

The statement reframed the problem *and* established a new *context* –a forgiving context. The CEO brought into play a sense of a cosmic relationship that transcended them all. Whereas before there had been emotions of anger and blame, suddenly there was a cosmic context. This new context put everyone on the same level. The heart of that context was a figure all identified as one who embodied love, forgiveness, and care.

The statement that all must "figure out what that means and how to make it work" called for a mutual development of the *instrument* that would make real the forgiving context in which the whole community would operate. Such a context, by definition of these past pages, was one that released the power for creativity through the whole organization.

At the end, some members of the staff surprised the interim CEO with not only a handshake but a hug. That "hug" was an instrument for the Council member but also became a new context for the CEO.

That was not the end of the story. The real test came at the first meeting of the Administrative Council chaired by the Interim.

A sensitive matter was on the agenda. The issue was the appointment of a new department head who was a racial ethnic minority. All believed in the ideal of inclusiveness. Some had concern that the woman in question lacked experience.

The CEO saw his role as facilitative. Debate ensued. The CEO sought to recognize each one who wished to speak and to make sure that each person's point was heard and clear. The discussion bogged down. Feelings began to rise.

In order to help the process and diffuse the tension, the CEO had an idea. He suggested the idea. Immediately, the dynamic changed. Every eye shifted to him. The shift was neither hostile nor friendly. It was direct. One person and then another addressed the CEO's suggestion strongly and negatively.

Finally, the CEO said, "Slow down. Don't you see what I am trying to do? Your discussion was getting nowhere. I threw out a suggestion to help focus–not a directive to tell you what to do."

And then paraphrasing a line from "Gone with the Wind," he said, "Frankly, my friends, I don't give a damn what decision you make. It's your decision."

A stunned silence ensued. One council member then said, "Yeah, I get it." After a short pause, the discussion started again – and within five minutes, a creative solution emerged. The affirmative vote was not unanimous but was substantial. The fact that some voted against the motion indicated the integrity of the process. All knew the will of the majority and also knew they had an honest difference of opinion – but a difference of opinion with which they could live.

After the meeting ended, council members left the room with animated conversation. One of them came back to the interim CEO who was picking up his papers and said, "I think that you should know what they are saying. They are marveling that they could come out of a meeting without being polarized. This has been a great beginning."

## *Discussion*

The word forgiveness never gets mentioned in this short description. Yet something happened that freed the council members sufficiently from past failures that they could make a creative decision. The emotions about the past were real. In this moment, the freedom to act creatively proved equally real.

From the *perspective of the observer*, we see the role of a cosmic context–the view that despite all the upsets, council members and CEO felt that they were in a context of care–God's care mediated through the meeting's process and the CEO.

The process had begun at the retreat. The experience at the meeting proved a first step in trying to "figure out" what it meant for the group to speak of being "in Christ" or having a "cosmic" head of the firm that transcended even the interim CEO. The action, based on that concept, emerged in the decision that was made AND in the conversation among committee members that followed.

In addition, an observer would note the room in which the meeting took place and the seating arrangement.

The Council met in a square room familiar to the members and the chair. For some time, the members had also sat in a large "U" shape. The CEO was familiar with that arrangement and the way it allowed people to see each other.

In line with field theory, this arrangement took seriously a view from what is called "Gestalt psychology." The view holds that a group of individuals is more than just the sum of the number of the individuals. In a group, a field dynamic results in something that is greater than adding all of the individuals together. This "something" effects every individual.

Equally, this arrangement allowed for empathetic moments. Everyone could see everyone else. Each brain could read each other's brains and seek to make some sort of integration.

We see here a good context for genuine interaction. The language of communication has many facets. Silence is itself a form of communication. A smile, a sparkle in the eyes, or a swinging of the legs can communicate a message. As people focus, the empathetic aspects of the brains come into play along with the memory dimensions. As various neurons fire in one person's brain, similar neurons fire in the brains of others.

However, none of these neurons fire in a vacuum. Jokes about "empty heads" are false. Each brain has its own inner and outer environment. Each brain seeks to integrate those neural firings with memories of similar events or past events. (I should say the perception of past events.) The brain needs to integrate (make sense of) these firings.

Given that overall structure, as sometimes happens in such groups, people could call for a time of prayer. An important dimension of that period of prayer is silence or meditation that allows these "firings" to do their job and allows the integration to become conscious. A Quaker meeting, for example, is designed to allow for this process. In such a meeting, there is silence, someone is moved to speak, as others empathetically get what is being said, there is more silence. Out of that silence, someone responds, and the process goes on.

*From the standpoint of the facilitator,* something happened when he made his suggestion. Almost everyone in the group seemed to challenge him. Why?

We remember from Hebbs Law that in certain situations, a dominant firing will always be accompanied by other dominant firings. That the new chair would make a suggestion triggered neurons that had developed when another CEO had made suggestions. Despite the fact of a new CEO with a new style, the field force brought into play the whole group of neurons that had fired in the past. That "firing" came regardless of the fact that the situation was different, this was the first meeting of the new CEO, and the reactions did not fit the circumstance.

This reaction says nothing about the accuracy or inaccuracy of the memory or the legitimacy of what past chairs have done or said. The reaction may simply indicate that old habits never die–at least without a fight. Such responses are the basis for neurosis. However, one would not get very far by telling the group to stop being neurotic! From the perspective of facilitation, the CEO had to deal with the reaction, but not in a way that insulted the group as a whole.

In this instance, almost instinctively, the chair took a different approach: By saying, "Don't you understand what I am doing," he barely got their attention. When this mild mannered and nice person who never shouts and never swears suddenly said with strength and emphasis, "I don't give a damn what you decide…" he got attention. In effect he said, "Listen."

Other responses have accomplished the same end. One might say in a very quiet voice, "Listen to yourselves, do you realize what you are doing?" That contrast of voice plus the question would have helped the group focus on its own process. As it was, we see only an implied "listen to yourselves." In this instance, the alternative approach worked because again it threw the focus back on the group. "It is your decision" keeps the focus on the group rather than allowing the group to blame the agent.

*The perspective of the ones facilitated* (or "the undergoer" to use Professor Feldman's word) first resulted in the group stopping for a moment to look at the process. In so doing, all backed off. People who had started to lean forward in their seats began to sit back. For a moment, no one said anything.

When the statement came, that the CEO simply wanted to redirect the focus in order to help the group, there was a moment of silence and then a member of the team said "Yea, I get it."

The process could not stop there nor did it. As the dominant neuron became neutralized, and people could look at the process, the group could then, AND DID begin to look at the problem in a new way. They came to a decision.

Finally, when the group dismissed and went out into the hall, they clarified with each other what in fact had happened. In so doing they affirmed each other and themselves.

*From the observer perspective*, again, in so doing they formed a new memory and a new neuron. That change created a context for all new discussion.

The dimension of caring also came into play. It became growingly clear that the chair cared about the group as a whole. The chair gave the context of care not only in the meeting but in the company as a whole. In that meeting, the healing process began.

1) It began in the difference between a strong shout that said "hear me" as opposed to an angry shout that said "I hate you." That context of care is a major dimension of the forgiveness experience.

2) The healing process of caring was mediated by the chair.

3) Equally important, the caring was received by the community and itself became the context in which it related to the chair. Thus, what was the instrument for the community became the context for others.

Earlier, we have said that the issues of justice and fair play are two of the issues in the whole area of forgiveness. Certainly at the point and time of this meeting, all had a feeling that the process was fair, and so was the decision – even though the vote was not unanimous. The dignity of every individual was affirmed as was the dignity of the group as a whole.

## *Forgiveness and the Survival of Oppression—a second event*

A common and understood response to oppression is simply this: "There is no God."

More than one victim of the Holocaust has said that he or she could not believe in a God who would allow to happen what happened to them or their families. Such people as I have known have sometimes been bitter or depressed or cynical. More often, the ones I have known well have been gentle, amazingly kind, and truly caring. Yet, they have given up on God. Who could not but understand the feeling?

Of equal interest are those who have had the same experience and become people of prayer, of social concern, and of profound faith. I mention three here:

A gentleman I will call Pastor Chen, served as a pastor of major church in Beijing.

Dr. Foldes, an ethnic Jew of Hungary and a Lawyer practiced law in his country.

Heinz Kappes of Germany, was an ordained Christian minister with broad ties to non-Christians – Jews, Moslems, Buddhists and Hindus.

(One might well ask why I do not have a woman in this sample. Indeed, I do know women who could be part of this sample. Unfortunately, I do not have their data in a recoverable form. I would point out, however, that the daughters of two of the men mentioned above are my resources for those men. These three events I know the best.)

I look at these experiences from the perspective of an observer.

Because he knew the U.S. Ambassador to China in the days of Chiang Kai Shek, Pastor Chen was arrested by the Maoist government in China.

Pastor Chen was sentenced to prison for ten years and sent to work in the mines. When the ten years were up, the "Red Guard" came into power in China, and put him in prison for another ten years. Finally when China moved out from under the rule of the "Gang of Four," he was freed and again took up his official role as a pastor.

When Margaret and I knew him, Pastor Chen served as one of the pastors of the church in Beijing attended by George H. W. Bush. The man who later would be President of the United States represented the United States during the opening of relations between the US and China under Richard Nixon. This church he attended, and of which

Pastor Chen was a pastor, was not an American church but a native Chinese church.

Pastor Chen's sermons were often laced with English so that others of us could follow the one hour presentations. When I asked Pastor Chen how he survived personally and emotionally he said, "I claimed the promise of the scripture which says, 'I am with you always, to the end of the age'" (Matthew 28:20).

This man lived a creative life even in prison. He took as his responsibility the care and emotional support of those imprisoned with him. My greatest memory of him is sitting at lunch and seeing waiters and waitresses coming up just to talk with him. Some had been part of the Red Guard themselves. Yet he attracted them with his empathy, his capacity for concern, and his genuine care. His action reminded me of Augustine's statement that one should offer forgiveness as ones gracious gift.

The second person is Dr. Foldes. Dr. Foldes was a Hungarian Jew for whom the life of Jesus had become most significant. As a Jew, he had seen his son-in-law taken off to die in Auschwitz. His wife had been imprisoned with other women and witnessed the worst of rape by German guards. Mrs. Foldes had been shot at with other women but survived because the pistol did not fire. She was the only survivor. Dr. Foldes himself had suffered.

When the war crimes trial came, a barber he knew well came to him greatly troubled. The barber's son had been one of those who did the killing. He asked Dr. Foldes to defend the son. Dr. Foldes raised the matter with his family at dinner. At first, all were stunned by the suggestion. They sat in silence. Mrs. Foldes then gave permission. Dr. Foldes and his family took the position that as Christians, they must exercise the practice of forgiveness. Dr. Foldes did everything possible for his young client. He presented appeals up to the last minute. The appeals failed and the young man was hung until he died.

The daughter, her son, Dr. Foldes and his wife later came to the United States and became part of the First Presbyterian Church of Forest Hills where I was pastor. Their lives had an impact on me as their pastor. Clearly, the process of forgiveness had had effects on them.

Their act allowed for ministry to a condemned man as he had to face death. It also allowed the Foldes family to put the experience of those horrible days sufficiently behind them that they could deal creatively with life ahead. Dr. and Mrs. Foldes died during my pastorate—and died surrounded by dignity and love.

The Foldes' daughter later married a doctor in New York. The two now move through retirement together. The Folde's grandson Matthew, holds a fine professorship in Brooklyn, New York, and has become a specialist in brain studies and psychoanalysis. That initial decision of forgiveness freed them emotionally for a full and active life.

The third person was the father of a woman who sang in the choir of the Fifth Avenue Presbyterian Church, New York, where I had been invited to preach. She, Elisabeth Watson, and her sister, Hildegard Wright, wrote an unpublished biography of their father, Heinz Kappes.

Heinz Kappes, born in 1893, grew up in a small German village in a family rich in the traditions of the arts. By all standards the family was economically poor but shared in the richness of the life of a small community. Heinz Kappes suffered imprisonment in both World War I and under the Nazis. He became an ordained minister and was a Christian socialist. His life and ministry centered in social work. He selected and emphasized ministry in the city to the poor. He spent time in India with a spiritual leader. He worked in Palestine with Jews and Palestinians alike. He related his commitment to the centrality of Jesus Christ and the mysticism he learned in India. In Palestine, he had a meaningful working relationship with Jewish leadership.

Under the Nazis, a key official in the church had him removed from the church because of his work and his stance against the Nazis. After the war, he went back to that same man who expelled him. The man received him with considerable nervousness. Heinz Kappes told him not to worry. He had not come for revenge. He practiced forgiveness. The man who betrayed him now had a role in the official reinstating of Heinz Kappes. The official also affirmed that Heinz Kappes had been right in his evaluation of Hitler.

From the perspective of an observer, we cannot tell from this story what was in the mind of the official that had first caused Heinz Kappes to be ousted from the ministry and then pushed for reinstatement. What is clear comes in the awareness that Mr. Kappes had a deep sense of the equality of all people before God. Even though he was ordained, his ministry was one of counseling and social work. He was not pastor of a church. For that reason he preferred not to be called "pastor". Nevertheless many sought his council even up to the last days of his life in 1988. At his death, he was lauded by many.

Two quotes are significant. The first is a statement from his time in prison:

"I want to mention an occurrence in prison in Pforzheim during my time there in 1933. After some days of quarrelling with my fate in this impenetrable development of my life, I saw one morning through the very high window in the wall the dawn light on the chimney of the dairy of Pforzheim: All the soot looked as if it had been gilded. From that time onward, I had the feeling that whenever there is something difficult in my life, the gold of heavenly light shines through." [65]

The second is a prayer he used in 1893 for a baptism of a child, Heinrich Martin. At the baptism, Heinz Kappes read these words:

"We greet you in the name of God, lovely boy, come to be with us on earth. We rejoice that you now belong to the Savior's flock. We know not what God has in store for your life. But this day we trust in His loving and gracious care. We thank Him who in His power and might answered your parents' prayers with such loving kindness. Grow and blossom under the banner of Christ; stand firm when the world rages around you and tries to tear it from your hands; follow the good shepherd, little lamb, even when the road becomes narrow and steep. May the prayerful wishes of your parents and godparents be fulfilled in your life. Become a light: Illumine the path to heaven for many: fight with courage and win the victory over life's darkness. May your road end in the glory of God's kingdom where, by His grace, we shall all be awaiting you."

In both these statements, we get a feel for Mr. Kappes' sense of the cosmic perspective for looking at life. More than that, through his own use of prayer, we see the discipline of making that perspective part of his daily operation in life. He spoke of the importance of forgiveness as part of the life style and direction of his life.

Surely, the only perspective from which any of us can read these stories is that of the observer. Yet, as we seek not only to observe from the outside but identify with the persons mentioned above, we are conscious that the oppressors in their lives did not have their best interests at heart. Yet, there was something that transcended all those oppressors– and that something was a tremendous sense of the cosmic that cared for them.

With Pastor Chen, that cosmic sense of care came through Jesus who promised always to be with him.

With Dr. Foldes, that sense of care came through a significant mediator, Jesus, whose words of forgiveness themselves became the model for his life--and for whom the living of that model became the instrument that made that forgiveness real.

With Mr. Kappes, the light which shone on the prison chimney mediated a context that "shines through" the horror of the day. As expressed in the baptismal prayer for young Heinrich, the hopes mediated by the child's parents and God parents can become the "light that illumines the path to heaven for many" and gives courage to "fight the good fight" of the moment.

In the lives of each of these, we see the context that showed itself in some form and then became real through an act of caring for those who came into their lives—fellow prisoners (Chen), one seeking a fair trial (Foldes), and the social concern for other individuals (Kappes).

We also can note that from the standpoint of brain studies, each decision was a choice, each decision resulted in creative action, and each action was possible because each could identify (empathize) with the situations faced.

## *Forgiveness and a Failed Moment of Care—a third event*

Here, I present a case that came early in my ministry. The story tells of a failure on my part. It may seem strange to report a failure! Yet, sometimes more can be learned from a failed moment than a successful one. Since this is not a book on counseling practice but on looking at different aspects of the dynamic of forgiveness, I find this "failure" frees one to look at our subject. This presentation is from the perspective of the change agent who failed.

As a relatively young minister, my family and I moved to a parish where I would be the sole pastor. The setting was residential but the church stood on a traveled street in Forest Hills, New York.

On this occasion, surrounded by boxes still unpacked, someone knocked on the church door. On opening the door, I found a couple that wanted to "meet the pastor." Caught off guard, I wondered how the couple had found me when I had just arrived. Still, I could not turn down this first request at the church. With apologies for the way things looked, I invited the couple to sit down.

After the usual pleasantries and delaying comments about the weather, the conversation went as follows:

>
> Minister:  Well, I gather you'd like to get married.
>
> Miss B:  Yes, we know that there are certain problems though.  What's the rule when a divorce is involved?
>
> Minister: (startled by the discovery of a divorce involvement)  Well, uh, technically the rule is that you can remarry after counseling and being sure that there is a readiness to marry again, but it all is pretty much left up to the discretion of the individual minister.
>
> Mr. A:  We have the papers here.  Would you like to see them?
>
> Min: Yes. Thank you. (The papers revealed that both people had been divorced.  One had been divorced three times on the ground of mental cruelty, and the other had been divorced twice on the ground of desertion.  The most recent divorce was four weeks old.)  I didn't realize how recently you had been divorced.
>
> Miss B:  Well, it is recent, but we had been separated for two years.
>
> Min: I see, (Pause) When would you want to get married?
>
> Mr. A. and Miss B:  Next week.
>
> Min: (Pause) Well, I just couldn't do it that soon.  In a situation like this, I would not be justified in going ahead without the approval of Presbytery.  It will be three weeks before the key committee meets.  I can take it up with them.  If it were a question of just one divorce, I would speak of a

time of counseling; but with this, I do not think I can make the decision. My hands are really tied.

Mr. A: We understand. (then sarcastically) We wouldn't want anyone to go against his regulations.

Min: If you wanted to wait and have me really go into this with you, I'd be glad to; but a week is just too soon.

Miss B: We'll think it over. In the meantime, thanks for your time.

Many things could be said about my obvious inexperience as a pastor, my newness to the role of being in charge, and the fact that I did not need to see anybody to tell me that this marriage was not a good risk. Yet, the various inadequacies help show up the areas of context, mediation and instrumentation.

To begin with, the context did not make the minister feel comfortable much less the couple. The minister was surrounded by everything that said "You are not ready for this." Further, the couple themselves did not convey any sense of a context for the minister in which he could really engage in conversation.

In fact, the minister's responses indicated the degree to which he was caught off guard and was not at peace with himself. The pauses indicate that mood. The lame excuse and ducking into the security of the church authorities showed it. And the response about needing Presbytery approval moved much too fast from the context to the matter of instrumentation.

Further, the response about needing approval said nothing about "care" of the couple. Indeed, the sarcastic response picked that up. The pastor never caught the signal and never did anything that communicated a sense of care.

One may well ask, "What was going on in his brain?"

From the model of the field, we can quickly see two things –
nothing empathetic clicked in either his brain or that of the couple.
Nothing allowed for a connection between them of his needs and
nothing allowed for an empathetic connection with their needs. All
sorts of other neurons were firing, but none that connected.

Basically, the minister was also unforgiving of himself. He was
angry at himself. The more he got into the conversation, the more poorly
he handled either the anger or the couple. The relationship got worse.
For the couple, the experience proved a disaster. The couple felt no
context from the minister that allowed them to express themselves and
to deal creatively with their problem. They saw their problem basically
as one of wanting to get married as soon as possible. Nothing happened
that would permit them to look at the problems.

As happens when the rational and emotional sides of the brain
have no freedom to operate, the situation moved down to the level of the
mid-brain where the issue was fight or flight. The minister's reference
to church authority was a form of flight. The sarcasm of Mr. A became
a form of fight. The final comment of Miss B returned to the matter of
flight, and they disappeared.

One of the values of the perspectival method comes in the basis it
gives for learning from a past experience. Here, for example, it is clear
that the organizational structure was not right. With unpacked boxes
all over the place, there was no freeing context for either that pastor or
the couple to operate.

We also see that there is something to the phrase, "heal thyself."
From the standpoint of the facilitator or the change agent, time needed
to be taken for becoming emotionally centered. The pastor's not being
centered resulted in an inability to communicate. What would have
happened, for example, had the pastor looked at the legal document
and simply said, "How do you feel about your past experiences with

marriage as you come to consider it yet again?" Such a response would have kept the matter centered on the couple's needs and not his needs.

What do we see when we raise the questions of justice or fairness? We must remember again that from a biblical standpoint, the word justice refers to right relations. We also need to remember that the issue of justice is also the issue of fairness. Much in life is not fair and much in life does not lead to good relations. In the context of many churches, the purpose of church law is both orderliness and the healing or redemption of the individual. Here, the minister was in part trying to get a sense of order in this mad rush to the altar. That aspect is good. On the other hand, the failure to establish any sort of right relation quickly dissolved the relation.

### *Forgiveness in Worship and Prayer—a fourth event*

In this section, we look at implications of this book for both community and private prayer.

The implications for both public and private worship have much in common and often overlap. Yet the dynamics of each are different. The reality of the field concept makes that inevitable.

Even in silent prayer, one person in silence becomes aware of a difference when just one other person comes into the same space even if that person remains silent. This phenomenon is so powerful that sometimes two people who have a close relationship with each other know that the other has entered a room before seeing or hearing a voice.

This difference can be enriching or annoying. It is annoying in something as relatively compact as walking the labyrinth. (A labyrinth is a circular map on a floor that one follows during a period of prayer.) In a larger space such as in the woods or in a large area such as a cathedral, the awareness of others also praying in silence gives a sense of oneness with a community of faith. Narrow the space, and the need for privacy often trumps the joy of fellowship. All of this is subjective and depends on the individual and the individual circumstance.

Therefore, let us look at two situations: one of public and the other of private worship: In doing so, I do not argue for any particular liturgy. I wish to show how the process of context, mediation, and instrumental action are needed for any valuable worship, and how that demonstrates a connection between forgiveness and prayer.

*Public Worship:* A particular city church is characterized by a genuine cross section of people – old and young, men and women, colors of all descriptions, street people and those from fine homes. The place is Denver, Colorado. Music plays as people enter. The worship begins formally when someone calls all to order and says, in effect, "Let us worship God."

On this particular occasion, the leader said, "God is a Spirit, and those that worship God must worship in Spirit and in truth."

The congregation responded with a hymn–the choice for this day began, "Morning has broken, like the first morning, …." The hymn spoke of God's creation.

After that introduction which asked for God's presence, the leader gave a call to confession. On this occasion she said, "What does the Lord require of us but to love justice, practice mercy and walk humble with our God? Yet each of us knows that we have come short of that goal. Let us therefore express our common confession and then, in silence, confess whatever we personally need to confess."

There are many confessions of sin. Sometimes this church uses the historic ones. On this day, however the newly written confession just quoted reflected the headlines of the day. The confessional statement read:

> "Oh Lord, we confess that we fall short of the goals
> we have set for ourselves much less those established in
> Scripture. A racial shooting took place in our city. We

neither condone nor believe in that, and yet, somehow, we have failed in our society to reach those who do. Forgive us by a cleansing of our minds and an opening of our hearts that we may know what to do and have the courage to do it. Amen."

There then came the period of silent reflection and private prayer for forgiveness of ways in which each individual had "missed the mark" in the prior days.

After the silence, the leader said, "Believe the good news of the Gospel, we are a forgiven people. Hallelujah, Amen."

There then followed a time when members of the congregation greeted each other with what is called "The exchange of the peace." One person would say to another, "The peace of God be with you." The other would reply, "And also with you."

Readings of the Bible and an anthem from the choir then followed. The music related to the scripture that would be read. The reading of the scripture was really another form of mediating or offering the context. Such a reading may also suggest action such as "feed my sheep."

The purpose of the sermon, then, was to "unfold" either the meaning of the context or the actions that make real the context. In China, where the sermon needs to educate people as to issues of daily living as much as the love of God, the sermon often takes forty-five minutes to an hour. That timing is necessary when both context and actions are given by the sermon.

When, however, the explanation is short, that explanation is generally called a "meditation" rather than a sermon.

On the occasion of this service of worship, the meditation was followed by a hymn that fit the theme of the sermon. In such an instance, the sermon usually tries to give a sense of the context of God's presence. And then the liturgy had another confession! Only this time the confession was, in effect, not a statement of what was wrong but of what was right.

Again, there are many such confessions from the historical experience of the church. Sometimes the confession is written for the occasion. In any event, this confession is called a "Confession of Faith" or an "Affirmation of Faith. On this occasion, the congregation recited an expression of what it believed by saying the Apostles' Creed.

Sometimes, a prayer is offered for the concerns of the people in the church and in the world. That prayer is an action often followed by an offering which should be designed to express the "moving on with life" that the instrument of action is.

The offering taken as an act of dedication to minister to the needs of the community and the world becomes that action. That offering is itself an instrumental act not just to collect money but to express ones relation to the community and to fellow worshippers.

A final hymn was sung. After the hymn, the leader challenged the people go out into the world and live in a way that reflected faith in God and God's love. With a final benediction (blessing), the time of worship ended and people went out into the world.

We find something of this flow in all liturgical churches. What may surprise people is that a dimension of this same flow is found also in evangelistic meetings and praise services. At least, it can be found if the service of worship takes seriously the interplay of the contextual and instrumental parts of the experience of forgiveness.

A context is always given such as in the singing of a hymn and an instrument of action is given such as in a prayer. On some occasions we have the time of worship which grows out of silence as in the Society of Friends (the Quakers).

The issue is whether or not the style of worship is done *properly and with understanding.*

What does it mean to be done properly? It means to be done with attention to the psychological rhythm that I just mentioned. That rhythm is as important as the theological framework that fits the groups observed.

Consider our daughter's church. She is a member of a Four Square Gospel Church. At one of her Sunday services of worship, I was fascinated to note a pattern to the praise songs. The songs were sung with a sense of order. The songs lead to prayer, the Scripture reading, and the sermon. The sequence of the songs included the same "psychological" rhythm of context and instrument that I have described in this book. When I noted that observation to the pastor, he fully agreed.

From the perspective of the *observer* the rhythm results in the capacity to be creative and to move on.

Look at the pattern in the example given here –

The call to prayer and the first hymn reflected the context of God's loving presence. In the presence of that love, all felt free to lift up what was wrong in their lives. All did it silently, but did it. Therefore, they had the confession that was made possible by the context.

As they moved from the call to worship through the public confession and the silent confession followed by the exchange of the peace, there were three levels of the context. The service had the cosmic, the community, and the personal levels. …After each level, there was an action appropriate to that particular context.

For the Hebrew and the Christian, the cosmic level spoke of the action of God in creation and mediated through Moses and the prophets. For the Christian, the action of God shows itself in the "new creation" that Paul saw in Jesus Christ. In fact, Jesus is spoken of not only as the Word of God, but by "word" we mean the "action of God."

On the community level everyone lives in a particular culture or mixture of cultures. Language is the chief expression of the cultural action. Every culture has a language or the variation of a language. The language has a base of neurons and procedures as Jerome Feldman and others have demonstrated. The environment of the culture has also influenced the development of those neurons and allowed others to die.

To know the culture, we study the language.

From the level of the ones *facilitated*, the difference in cultures raises the question: *What are the actions that bring alive a context for one person and becomes the context in which another person then lives?*

The phrase in the Lord's Prayer, "Forgive us our debts as we forgive our debtors," gives us a clue. The act of forgiveness itself, as said before, becomes an instrument that makes forgiveness real to the forgiver as well as to the forgiven. Yet that is not enough to say.

In one culture, for example, laying a hand on a child as a blessing means a great deal. The Bible speaks of the laying on of hands as a form of dedication, of setting a person aside for special work, and so on. In some cultures in India, however, the laying of a hand on a child gets associated with a curse. It carries a worse connotation than even that of angrily shaking ones fist at another. Or in the area of language, the use of the formal or the informal greeting can suggest a sense of worth or lack of worth.

The liturgy developed in this section is a western means of trying to develop the rhythm in which the power of forgiveness becomes realized. Every culture and every group needs to do that for itself. As time goes on, and new generations come along, other words or rituals may be needed for that same realization of forgiveness.

From the perspective of the *facilitator* or the *agent*, all of this presents a basic problem - execution. The leadership execution of what is outlined above takes understanding, training, and experience.

We can know all the theory, follow all the rules that relate to worship, and end with a complete failure. Surely we have attended lectures, dramas, movies, and different types of service of worship that left us cold. As one person said of a particular service of worship, "That service had no soul."

The fact is that each of us needs people who can coach us in the actual conduct of a counseling session, a class session, or a service of worship. If we do not know how to communicate with our whole being, not just our minds and our words, all the "correctness" goes for naught. A leader who seeks to mediate the context of forgiveness needs to look at any event from the perspective of his or her particular style. A mediator learns how, given that style, to communicate integrity, understanding, vulnerability, and a sense of caring.

Such does not come from reading a book – including this one. Such communication comes only with experience and practice where a person can learn how he or she appears to others.

*Private Worship:* In the matter of private prayer, the concern for "context" means that one looks for a place conducive to prayer or that one creates the context in the place where he or she is.

For some people, the sea shore with the crash of ocean waves is the place to be, for another, a spot high in the mountains gives the answer. A special place in Muir Woods near the San Francisco Bay became the spot for the architect of the Golden Gate Bridge. A temple becomes "the place" for some and the quiet of the Friends meeting house answers the need for others.

If one cannot get to a special place, the late D.T. Niles of Sri Lanka and India taught his students to close their eyes and imagine a serene spot that was familiar. Pray in that context.

Others have followed the practice of Ignatius of Loyola by reading a story of the Bible, imagining that he or she was in the scene, picturing Jesus as coming near and of having a conversation with Jesus.

Those in the Orthodox tradition learn the art of "gazing" at an icon – not studying it but gazing at it – and letting the feel of that gaze become the context. Those who use the mantra do so in part because it creates a sound that sets a context.

In his article on prayer for the American Bible Society years ago, John Sutherland Bonnell of Canada and New York spoke of reading a passage of Scripture until a verse "hit home." One would then memorize that verse, say it quietly, and let the verse be the context for the time of prayer.

A key element in private prayer has to do with "letting go" or "emptying oneself." A person should first stretch and squeeze the muscles of the body. That physical form of "emptying" should be followed by an emptying of the mind. By allowing thoughts to come into the mind and letting them go, one slowly empties the mind. Feelings of guilt, failure, shame, should be part of that. Some people even write them down and then burn the paper. Many use the "Jesus prayer" by saying "Have mercy on me O Lord, a sinner." As this phrase is repeated slowly, again and again, more softly and more softly, one empties himself or herself.

And then one seeks to listen. Biofeedback tests indicate that in such a period, the most creative brain waves come alive in the brain.

In all of this, private prayer is as much a listening as it is a speaking. At the end of the time, one considers the tasks of the day and moves out into them.

From the perspective of the observer, any form of private prayer or meditation flows from context to an instrument of action consistent with the experience of the meditation. These two parts ("poles" to use the technical word) of the field allow for a free flow within ones spirit that allows for creativity and growth.

From the perspective of the *agent* or *facilitator*, the task is to guide and help with understanding, but not to take the place of the Spirit.

From the perspective of the one *facilitated,* the need is for the time and the repetition that allows neurons to be strengthened. When issues arise, we want to have developed clusters of constructive neurons that fire and give one an inner power.

## *Forgiveness and the Funeral—a fifth event*

When we come to forgiveness and the funeral, study of the brain suggests that once again we deal with two fields at once – the field of the brain and the field of the group.

For the purpose of this section on practice, however, I focus on the matter of the individual's grief and the group grief to which the funeral seeks to minister.

In the reality of grief, there will be similarities amongst individuals and there will be differences. Some will have come to the service of worship out of respect. Others, especially family members, will have come out of a sense of loss–deep loss. For the group as a whole, there will be feelings of loss for the group.

> The question for preparation of the funeral is: "What kind of service of worship will bring healing in the grief or sense of loss, forgiveness of the guilt or inadequacy, celebration of the life that has been lived, and direction and hope for the future – whatever that future may be?

Let us begin with what has happens to the brain of the worshipper at a funeral. If we could take a person at the moment of learning about a death, surely there would be evidence of activity in all parts of the brain. The cognitive side of the brain would seek to make sense out of all that has happened. Different parts of the mid-brain would try to deal with a myriad of matters – memories that swarmed from different parts of the past and thus different parts of the brain; awareness of inadequacies, sin, failure, the "if only" thoughts. Suddenly there might be a moment of laughter – where did that come from in this moment of the funeral? Out of the memories, a funny moment and a time of joy come to the surface. ...And then may come the thought "This will never happen again." The worshipper becomes aware of a new sadness.

The sadness when recognized, then leads to a new joy with awareness that one is stronger for the time shared and now remembered.

In the moments after the death of another, a certain numbness, an "I can't believe it," and a loss of any direction may come both to a community and to an individual. By the time of the funeral, some have moved beyond the initial numbness. Other issues will have surfaced. Maybe anger has become strong. Others will feel terribly alone.

For the pastoral leadership at the funeral, there is a legitimate pattern that may be followed formally or informally. I find it helpful to divide this process into areas of:dealing with grief and guilt or shame, celebrating the life, and moving on to new life.

There is a tendency in looking at death to see these as three separate stages through which we pass. It seems logical to deal with the grief, put that behind us and move on to the next stage.

Our experience with the field theory, however, should correct any such assumption. The experience of these three dimensions all shift simply because we are dealing with a process that is more than three dimensional and more than a matter of tapping into this wire or turning off that nerve connector. Although a drug may help, drugs seldom foster the process. Most drugs help only to ignore the process.

From our knowledge of how a field process works, we know that there will be ebbs and flows with the ultimate result of healing and wholeness. There will be the yin and the yang.

The pastoral leader must clarify whether or not he or she is an observer, an agent, or the one needing ministry for his or her own feelings. The truth is that that at various moments, a pastor is any one of these. The first step is to recognize the reality and deal with it.

A particular pastor had to give the meditation at the funeral of another pastor who was a key leader and in the prime of life. He recognized that and began by saying, "I do not know about you folks, but right now I am angry." His speaking to that feeling for a moment then freed him to move into the facilitative (agent) role of helping the congregation deal with their moment of anger. After that particular funeral a daughter spoke to the pastor. His own sense of loss was considerable, but she did not begin with that. Instead she said to the pastor, "I am proud of the way you have handled this for us and all that have come."

Consider the shifts that took place in that moment for her compliment to the pastor. With that comment, she affirmed him. In the midst of his feelings of inadequacy, she put him in touch with another dimension of himself. For a brief moment, she ministered to him

We are all part of the field of the process and different parts of that field emerge at different moments and in any particular moment. That having been said, there are times when any one of these dimensions – the grief, the celebration, the hope – is dominant. The pastor or service leader needs to be alert as to which dimension is dominant and address it.

That is why, as said at the outset, I divide the time of the service of worship into the three sections. Yet, in the conduct of the service of worship itself, there may always be a repeat of a past emotion in the midst of a succeeding one. The one who conducts the service must be prepared to deal with that shift.

In addition, some traditions recognize much better than the western that grief does not end with the funeral. The Jewish tradition has its regular times of prayer for the year that follows the death. The Chinese tradition has a service of worship on the anniversary of the death every year for three years. In the Korean culture people have an annual period of travel to a family grave to honor those who have died.

For those interested, I have outlined in the attachments an order for a service of worship and burial.

## Conclusion

As we look at the practical application of forgiveness, we see that forgiveness is a process which, when practiced, leads to the power for creativity. Such a power is needed in the world and essential in the lives of us all.

May we all practice the art of that forgiveness and know of that power.

# Epilogue – Concluding Reflections

In the course of preparing this material, several suggestions have come as to topics friends and colleagues hoped I would include. Subjects such as meditation, conflict resolution, and healing require books in and of themselves. I hope that here I have laid a foundation for those areas of concern by lifting up the initial role of the dynamic of forgiveness.

## *Implications for any Christian Community of Faith*

For those of us in the Christian tradition, Christ is seen as the mediator and the church is seen as the "body of Christ." That means any Christian community of faith must provide the context in which the process of forgiveness can move ahead. That also means any Christian community of faith must take those actions which make the process of that forgiveness real to all – to themselves and to others.

Historically, that meant attention to the "sacred space" in which people gathered. One part of that "sacred space" has to do with architecture. Sacred space has a role as we think of context.

1) Hagio Sophia in Istanbul today is a mosque. Called one of the "seven wonders of the world," Hagio Sophia is noted for a dome that was the first built with windows around the base that permitted light to shine down on those below. Early on, Christian sanctuaries were simply copies of government halls at which one end had the altar. This fit the western concept of guilt and justice. In Hagio Sophia – with the influence of the "near-East" that changed. Here, the focus centered on the people in the center. The architecture itself allowed light to shine on each one and gave a freedom to be oneself in

that space and at that time. The context of that space was a forgiving context.

2) A simple, white Quaker meeting house in Westchester County had a similar result. The seating arrangement permitted people to face each other. Each one was free to speak as "the Spirit" moved. No matter what one wore, how one looked, how one felt, all were accepted as a "Friend" and free to listen or to speak. The community in that sacred space created a context of forgiveness and a freedom to make real that forgiveness and wholeness.

3) A modern example of sacred space in architecture is next to the concentration camp in Dachau, Germany. A Roman Catholic Church stands outside the wall where it was during the holocaust. The church had to be rebuilt. The interior is all in white. As one stands at the back pew and looks up to the chancel area, the alter is in white with markings that reminded me of a cellblock. Behind the alter on the white wall is not a crucifix with the dead body of Christ, but a great cross. The crown of thorns made as barbed wire winds around the cross. The effect reminded one of crucifixion, tragedy, and resurrection all in one. Even more, it reminded one of the context of love – for no one "has greater love than this but to give life for a friend." We stood in sacred space indeed.

4) At the forming of the United Nations, there initially was a prayer room. In the center of the room, there was the base of a tree with green leaves surrounding it. Here, in this space, there was that which said, "anyone may come" and everyone can be surrounded by the sense of new life from the stump. Sadly, that is not there anymore, but the recognition of the

sacred space shown in architecture stood as a great symbol.

As the pastoral care movement rose to a professional level in the 1950s, attention was given to the role of context. Carl Rogers, John Sutherland Bonnell, Frieda Fromm Reichmann, Seward Hiltner and Lowell Colston all paid attention to context. They also spoke to the matter of space. We need to recover that sense in the spiritual lives of each of us as individuals with our individual "fields of force" and in the life of the faith community with the community "field of force."

Where is the action that makes this context real? It comes in the act of so dealing with another that he or she may find himself or herself in a sacred space – a space that releases the power to be creative. When we have that power, we have the practice of forgiveness.

Let us therefore go forth to be those people for a world in which the discipline of forgiveness becomes the method of healing the brokenness of this day.

# Attachment One

## *The Search for Appropriate Instruments Today*

As one looks around the world at different cultures and different ways of doing things, many and different instruments emerge out of different cultures. Each of these approaches allow the context of forgiveness to come alive – and with it the ability to live not just in reaction to the world about us, but in creative response.

One of my personal concerns lies in the tendency to copy western cultures in the East or to bring Eastern practices into the West because they are different and not because they help. It takes time to understand how and why a particular instrument works. One cannot just use an act of instrumentation simply because it worked for another person in another context.

An experience in India gives an example:

At the United Theological College and Seminary in Bangalore, worship is conducted regularly. Because the school reflects the presence of people from many cultures in India, students are invited to set up a liturgy that fits their cultures.

On one occasion, that meant using the main floor to have a beautiful design made with leaves and flower blossoms. As one watched the students arranging the pedals and then placing a candle lit on a holder of Indian design, one could sense those preparing come alive. The work of setting up the context for others made the context real to those who did the work.

When the time for worship came, we all just sat and absorbed the design. Soon, we heard the sounds of the Tabla as the drummers began a steady rhythm. In the course of time, scripture was read, a meditation given, prayers offered. The sermon helped mediate to us the context and in that freedom, we moved out after the benediction to the work of the day.

In that setting, in that time, the process of forgiveness came alive and opened up the possibility and power to act creatively. When some of us took the process to the United States, however, what had been an experience of worship became a show. The acts of instrumentation were not acts that grew out of our culture and our experience.

At a Benedictine monastery near Providence, Rhode Island, the setting was different. In that community of priests, the visitor shared the full life of the monastery routine. The feature was the balance of prayer and work. Five times in the day, we had worship in the chapel. Here, one found a sense of being in the context of God's forgiving presence. Here, after the benediction, we all moved out to our work – the instrument that made the context real.

After a few hours, we returned again to contemplate what had been done, to confess where we had fallen short, to hear the assurance of pardon, and to go out again with the past behind us – made the more real by facing new issues with new creativity.

Thus, the rhythm prevailed that took us from context, to context mediated, and to context made real by the instrumentation of our work. One became aware of these times of clearing the brain, of renewal in ones whole being, and of the creativity of God – in us.

Another feature of today is the interest in the Gnostic Gospels.

News articles on the life of Professor Elaine Pagels of Princeton have reported that it was in the study of the Gnostic Gospels that she rediscovered her faith. What the difference was Professor Pagels expresses in her own works. What I see in some of them is an attempt to make forgiveness real.

At that time in Professor Pagels life, the theological accuracy of the gospel accounts was not the issue. Theological or political correctness were not the point. The point was, "Why have they helped her and others?"

Part of the value of the Gnostic writings comes in the title of a book by the late Robert MacAfee Brown of Stanford Univesity: *Seeing the Gospel with Third World Eyes.*

Too often, we become so jaded by the ills of our own or another culture that we cannot see the truths that that culture may be hiding. In Bob Brown's book, it is clear that one does not just go to a third world and see anew. One has to become enough a part of that thinking to sense the truth or error in that thinking. From what we learned about empathy, it is necessary to take the time for the brain cells developed in one culture to connect with the brain cells of people in another culture. When we get those "third world eyes" we see something we did not see before. It seems to me that the Gnostic Gospels may also do just that.

To say that one can learn from the Gnostic Gospels, however, does not mean that they become any substitute for the Bible.

I also wish to say a word about the concept of a "Church Mother."

Professor Elsie Anne McGee of Princeton Theological Seminary has introduced us to Katharina Schütz Zell of Strasburg. She and her husband contributed much to the Reformation, and Ms Schütz Zell's work went on long after her husband's death.

Katharina Schütz Zell saw herself as a "church mother."

This idea of a "church mother" means far more than a sentimental description of a fine woman. For her, it was a concept which, according to Dr. McGee, came to young Katharina at the age of ten. It developed through the years and became particularly strong after the death of her husband. For her, the role had a particular emphasis on witness and on teaching.[66]

As a result, Katharina Schütz Zell had a major part in the discussion of the sacrament of communion. In that discussion, she stood with those who had a sense of the "real presence" in that sacrament rather than just a memorial. The teaching shows up again in her pamphlets and books and in the life she lead as a teacher not just of women but of pastors themselves.

The value of the concept of a "church mother" lies in raising up a part of the feminine in the kind of context needed in the context of the church community. It helps give a balance that often has not been there in the patriarchal approach of much of western Christianity.

We cannot mention Katharina Schütz-Zell in the Europe of the Reformation without also mentioning a similar approach in India today.

There, the role of the "church mother" is taken seriously with full liturgy and recognition.

# Attachment Two

## *The Memorial or Funeral Service of Worship*

At any moment of any memorial service of worship and at any of the three sections mentioned in the section on practice, several types of experience need recognition –

The moment of grief over a sense of loss; the moment of memory – memory of that for which one feels ashamed and memory of that for which one feels a sense of grace; the moment of celebration; the moment of closure and moving on.

These moments are easily identified. What is not so easy to identify is when these moments will turn on and off again in the course of a funeral service, a memorial service, or the burial.

Eg. the sense of loss needs the balance of a sense of closure and moving on, and the moment of memory needs the moment of celebration. The moment of grief needs recognition again and again.

The reverse also is true – the moving on will not work if there is not clarity as to what now is in the past; the celebration has no meaning if we have no memory of that which we really are celebrating.

The actual service of worship then is aware of several levels of activity. The following is an example:

First level –

The first level probably begins with the meeting and gathering of family and friends as they enter the place of worship together. This level certainly is operative when we have the call to worship, invocation and/or opening hymn. These establish the context in which the service begins.

Whatever is done, including the quiet but welcoming silence of the Quaker meeting, mediates the context of love.

The confession of need (or sin) becomes the next step.

As when one goes to the doctor or counselor and hears the friendly, "What is on your mind," we practically never respond with what is fine. We say what is bothering us. Often at a funeral, that need is awareness that we cannot control everything and that there are powers and forces in life greater than any of us. It may indeed be confession of a sin, a failing, a missing the mark.

The next step is assurance that we are a forgiven people and all the people are forgiven individuals.

The "assurance of pardon" in Christian liturgies is more than the conclusion of the first level. The "assurance" is another mediating of the context – only now we have it at a deeper level than at the first.

The instrument of action that follows this level is sometimes what I spoke of as "the sharing of the peace" in which people greet each other and say anything from "good morning" to "the peace of God be with you."

At other times there may be a song, or at still other, a reading of Scripture. In some settings, the action may be one of silence – a silence that allows what has just been said fully to be absorbed by all involved.

Personally, I like to have Psalms or certain passages from the Hebrew Scriptures read here. These serve as actions that help one "own" the reality of the forgiveness and at the same time become the new context for moving on.

In a full service, a hymn or a special musical presentation becomes a response that allows for this level to be personally owned and sets the context for going to a deeper level.

After this cycle, readings from the Christian Scriptures or special readings of poetry, or sections of scripture–particularly of the resurrection for those who are Christian – mediate the context once again at yet another level of depth.

Again, the response of a hymn or another presentation of music become the instruments of action and set the context for a spoken word.

However it is done, this "spoken word" means a meditation that mediates the context again–only this time at a deeper level than before.

Here, what is sometimes called a "eulogy" really is a means of helping the brain remember – particularly remember the loss, the good times that will be missed, the bad times that must be put behind.

Here also, in what is often another form of meditation, we bring up memories at a deeper level than at the beginning. Dietrich Bonheoffer is attributed with the statement, "Preaching is telling people what they already know." Whether it is the memory of the risen Christ or the memory of some great truth, the purpose here is to bring to conscious awareness that which is of strength that may have been buried by the fears or sorrows or confusions of the death,

The "instrument of action" that follows is some statement of affirmation. This "instrument" can then become the context for the sacrament of the Eucharist (communion) as in those traditions that use that sacrament in such a service of worship. Where there is no burial service – in the earth or at the sea – a form of committal helps to bring closure.

Given what we have learned about the interplay amongst different parts of the brain, the benediction needs to be done is such a way as to indicate not just that the funeral service is over but that we have a task to do as we go forward.

Therefore, a charge may be given such as, "Let us go forth resolved that we will live in such a way that this life will not have been lived in vain." After World War I, the poem from Flanders Field was often used with words that read, "To you from failing hands we throw the torch, be yours to hold it high....if you break faith with us who die, we shall not sleep, though poppies grow in Flanders field."

If the burial or committal of ashes come at a different time and place from the service of worship, we need to remember that all those dynamics that were part of the memorial service itself continue.

For that reason, I begin the time of burial with a reading from the book of Revelation which speaks of the new heaven and the new earth and of the New Jerusalem that is for us. These sections from Revelation 21 and 22 portray that new creation which makes real the forgiveness which we understand as such freedom from bondage to the past that we may live creatively in the days ahead.

In the context of that affirmation, we then may lower the casket or spread the ashes.

Some traditions have individuals take a shovel and share in putting earth into the grave. The final benediction gives closure.

# Attachment Three

## Forgiveness in the Moment of Meditation

Two more historic processes of prayer and meditation and one modern process deserve special mention. Each of these takes seriously the rhythm of forgiveness: context, mediation of the context, action that makes the context real to oneself and others:

## The Cloud of Unknowing

The process that I find most identifies with what I have said here is the *Cloud of Unknowing*. I commend this fourteenth century book. It speaks of the ultimate goal of oneness with God. The steps it identifies are those of reading, thinking, and prayer. The "Cloud" calls these steps "Lesson, Meditation, and Orison." *(The Cloud of Unknowing: a shortened version*...Harper and Row, New York, 1948, p. 21) Note how the total experience uses different fields of the brain. Note also that the process begins with reading which establishes a context. (As would also a lecture, a sermon, or a picture.)

The brain processes what is read and thus mediates the context in which we function.

The act of prayer is an act, usually of surrender to the context as understood, in which we both speak and listen. That act becomes the instrument that makes the context real.

## *Ignatian Spirituality*

The Ignatian practice makes marvelous use of the imagination. One way of following that practice comes when the individual imagines a passage in Scripture - such as Jesus with the disciples by the shore. The individual imagines Jesus coming toward him or her and having a conversation. Out of that silence, the experience is then often shared with another as a way of clarifying and testing the meaning of the experience itself.

## *Alcoholics Anonymous*

Those familiar with Alcoholics Anonymous meetings will note much of the same rhythm in the process of the AA meeting itself. The group gives a context of forgiveness. The members tell their stories. The group accepts the person with his or her story. The twelve steps of AA then indicate the means of action that ultimately make real the context.

# Attachment Four

## Bibliographic Resources

Although this short book does not need an index, I submit the following list of authors and books as a resource base for those who wish to pursue the direction of this book. Various professional journals of the scientific community are a basic resource: eg. *Science, Scientific American, The New England Journal of Medicine. Pastoral Psychology, The Journal of Pastoral Care.* In addition, books on the social dimension and the discipline of love by people such as Martin Luther King and Bishop T. H. Ting of China are paramount.

Some of the books listed here are not referred to in the body of this work. However, all of them, such as the work by Alfred North Whitehead, have informed the basic thinking out of which I write.

So that one may judge what books will or will not be helpful to those who wish further exploration of the subject in this book, I give a one line comment that indicates the point at which I found the book particularly helpful.

Research in this world of the brain continues at fast pace. When Dr. Leonard Rosenman passed his scientific journals on to me he said, "Remember, anything you read today is just a hypothesis." As the latest of several examples, he gave me an article just before this book went to press.

That article appeared in *Science* volume 316, April 6, 2007. On page 57, Larry R. Squire of the Department of Psychiatry, Neurosciences and Psychology, University of California, San Diego VA Medical Center wrote about memory. He spoke of a "schema" that referred to "pre-existing knowledge structures into which newly acquired information can be incorporated." One schema helps with memory consolidation. In this book, we spoke of the hippocampus as the place where facts and events were remembered. That still holds. Yet, the new research shows that a process of memory consolidation establishes those memories in distributed regions of the neo-cortex. Those established structures allowed for quick establishment of new material that removed dependence on the hippocampus.

That information has interesting implications for the field dynamic spoken of here, for understanding the process of experiencing forgiveness, and for the role of training in this or that faith and ethic as one grows. This is not the place to pursue the discussion. This is the place to underscore the importance of the role of forgiveness in a life that is creative.

I submit the following list of resources for as a partial base for this continuing exploration.   .

Ali, Carroll A. Watkins, *Survival & Liberation: Pastoral Theology in African American Context.* Chalice Pres, St. Louis, 1999. Dr. Watkins Ali demonstrates the use of the perspectival method in studies of the African-American context.

Allport, Gordon W., *Personality—A Psychological Interpretation,* Henry Holt and Co., New York 1937. Here we have an easily read overview of thought on personality that moves beyond the work of William James.

_____*Becoming: Basic Considerations for a Psychology of Personality,* Yale University Press, New Haven, 1955. Dr. Allport's classic introduces the concept of the "proprium."

Bass, Diana Butler, *Christianity for the Rest of Us,* Harper, San Francisco, CA, 2006. The three chapters on transformation relate well to the issues of "instrumentation" in forgiveness.

*Benedict, The Rule of* Trans. By Cardinal Casquet, Cooper Square Publishers, N.Y. 1966. This publication gives a concise, clear translation of the *Rule.*

_____1980, Editor Timothy Fry, OSB, The Liturgical Press, Collegeville, Minnesota, 1980. This book, prepared for the fifteen hundredth anniversary of the traditional date for St. Benedict, is a thorough documentation not only of monasticism but of how principles discussed in the prior pages have been used throughout the centuries.

Blakemore, Susan, *Consciousness: An Introduction,* Oxford University Press, NY. 2004. This book is based on her course work and written for students in any form of "Brain studies 101."

Bary, William A., & Connolly, William J., *The Practice of Spiritual Direction,* Seabury Press, NY, 1982. One form of spiritual direction.

Bulkeley, Kelly - *The Wondering Mind,* Routledge, New York, 2005. This book could well become a classic in its portrayal of the dynamic of the brain.

*John Calvin Writings on Pastoral Piety,* Trans. By Elsie Anne McKee, The Classics of Western Spirituality, Paulist Press, New Jersey, 2001. Calvin's "Preface to the Psalms," with its understanding of worship, prayer, and practice, gives insight that relates to the discipline of forgiveness.

Cameron, Catherine, *Resolving Childhood Trauma,* Sage Publications,, Oakland, CA, 2005. Along with the book by Cooper-White, this book gives an excellent study of the issues of trauma and means of coping.

Community Service Society of New York, *Report of the Study Committee to the Board of Trustees of the Community Service Society of New York,* Published by CSS, NY. 1971   As the basic author of much in this report, I list this material and its accompanying research as evidence of the community dimension in forming the context of forgiveness.

Cao, Tia Yu, *Conceptual Developments of 20$^{th}$ Century Field Theories,* Press Syndicate of the University of Cambridge, Cambridge University Pres, 1997. Tian Yu Cao gives a heady but remarkable study of different types of fields of force and the philosophical implications of field theory.

Chan, Wing-Tsit, *A Source Book in Chinese Philosophy,* Princeton University Press, Princeton, N.J. 1963. This excellent source book gives not only a sense of basic tenants of the Tao with its "yin and yang" or Confucian thought but also of the development of these views throughout the centuries.

Goleman, Daniel, *Destructive Emotions: How Can We Overcome Them: A Scientific Dialogue with the Dalai Lama,* Bantam Books, 2003, N.Y. Although the research in this book deals with brain activity in the course of meditation, much here also relates to the dynamic of forgiveness.

Cooper-White, Pamela,-*The Cry of Tamar, Violence Against Women and the Church's Response,* Fortress Press, Minneapolis, 1995. The discussion of forgiveness in relation to rape is realistic, practical, and clear about what forgiveness is not as well as what it is.

Corrigan, John, Editor, *Religion and Emotion: Approaches and Interpretations,* Oxford University Press, 2004. Although most of us turn to Joseph Le Doux as the authority on emotion and brain studies, this book gives the work of various authors and thus brings different perspectives on how emotions work.

D'Aquili Eugene and Newberg, Andrew, *The Mystical Mind, Probing the Biology of Religious Experience*, Fortress Press, Minneapolis, 1999. As one of the first books I read in this area, I still find this book a good introduction to brain studies and spiritual experience.

Dunbar, Flanders, *Mind and Body: Psychosomatic Medicine.* Random House, NY. 1947 This book should remind us that scholarly awareness of the body/mind concept has a helpful history of examination.

Emerson, James, *The Dynamics of Forgiveness,* Westminster Press, Philadelphia, 1964 As this current book has centered on brain studies and forgiveness, the former book centered on the use of psychological research developed in Client-Centered Therapy and forgiveness.

_____, *Divorce, the Church, and Remarriage,* Westminster Press, Philadelphia, 1961. This book became part of the change of main line denominations in the approach to marriage where a prior divorce had been involved. Forgiveness became key to the process of preparation for remarriage.

_____, *Suffering: Its Meaning and Ministry,* Abingdon Press, Nashville, 1986. This book adds the dimension of personal and group suffering to the discussion of forgiveness.

Enright, Robert D and Fitzgibbons, Richard P, *An Empirical guide for Resolving Anger and Restoring Hope*, American Psychological Association, Washington DC 2000, Fifth Printing, 2006. This is a remarkable book from top minds in the field.

Erdelyi, Matthew Hugh, "A Unified Theory of Repression" in *Behavioral and Brain Sciences, (2006) 29, pp 499-551* As a "scholar's scholar," Dr. Erdelyi offers a view of repression that enlarges our understanding of memory as a whole even as it focuses on repressed memory.

Feldman, Jerome, *From Molecule to Metaphor-A Neural Theory of Language,* Massachusetts Institute of Technology, *2006.* This excellent book on language develops the perspectival method as a scientific method that is essential for research in many forms of human relations - including the relationship of forgiveness.

Gershen, Kaufman, *Shame: The Power of Caring,* Schenkman Books, Inc., Rochester, VT., 1980 This comparatively short treatment of "shame" has the virtue of seeing the positive as well as the negative dimensions of shame in experience.

Hamilton, James, *A Life of Discovery, Michael Faraday, Giant of the Scientific Revolution,* Random House, NY 2002 This excellent biography of one who influenced Planck and Einstein brings Faraday into the discussion of today's concerns.

Hiltner, Seward, *Preface to Pastoral Theology, The Ministry and Theory of Shepherding;* Abingdon Press, N.Y., and Nashville, 1958. The *Preface* gives the first thorough discussion of the perspectival method of research when used for religious-particularly Christian-communities of faith.

Hogue, David, *Remembering the Future, Imagining the Past* Pilgrim Press, Cleveland, 2003. Amongst many genuine insights, the author's work on memory and his application of the lessons from brain studies that relate to worship, make this important for those who lead worship services.

Johnson, Steven, *Mind Wide Open: Your Brain and the Neuroscience of Everyday Life,* Scribner, N. Y., 2004. This popular writing takes the author through his own experiences of magnetic imaging for understanding the process of his own brain.

Junying, Geng and Zhuhong, Su, *Practical Traditional Chinese Medicine & Pharmacology: Basic Theories and Principles,* New World Press, Beijing, China, 1990. This book gives a brief but good presentation of the yin and yang in Chinese medicine and thought.

Koch, Christof, *The Quest for Consciousness - A Neurobiological Approach,* Roberts and Co. Publishers, Englewood, CO, 2004. This brilliant book by a colleague of Francis Crick has become basic for discussing the matter of consciousness.

Lao Tzu, *Tao Teh Ching,* John C. H. Wu, translator, Shambhala, Boston, 1989. This book is a fine translation that has the Chinese characters and the English translations on facing pages.

LeDoux, Joseph, *The Emotional Brain: The Mysterious Underpinnings of Emotional Life,* Touchstone Books, Simon and Schuster, N. Y. 1996. A basic book that relates the emotional and the cognitive in the brain.

Lewin, Kurt (Cartwright, Dorwin, Edit.) *Field Theory and Social Science;* Harper & Row, New York, 1951 This book is a compilation of the basic contribution made by Kurt Lewin to our understanding of field theory in a social setting.

Lewis, Michael, *Shame: The Exposed Self,* The Free Press, N.Y. 1992. The title expresses the contribution of this book - namely the dynamic of shame as that of being discovered (exposed).

Libet, Benjamin, *MindTime: The Temporal Factor in Consciousness,* 2004, Harvard, Cambridge, Mass., 2004. As years ago Carl Heim spoke of needing to understand time and space in more than three dimensional ways, Dr. Libet demonstrates the implications of that view.

McCullough, Michael E.; Pargament, Kenneth I. Thoresen, Carl E.; Editors, *Forgiveness,: Theory, Research and Practice;* The Guilford Press, N.Y. 2000. One of several remarkable books sponsored by the Templeton Foundation.

McKee, Elsie Anne, *Katharina Schütz Zell: The Life and Thought of a Sixteenth Century Reformer,* Vol. I, Brill, Boston, 1999. Dr. McKee has given us a rare insight into a woman reformer whose understanding of spiritual dynamics helps illumine aspects of the dynamic of forgiveness.

McKnight, John; *The Careless Society: Community and Its Counterfeits,* Basic Books N.Y.I 995. Although this book does not speak of forgiveness as such, it does picture a basic problem of society that needs a creative and not reactionary response.

McNeill, John T., *The History and Character of Calvinism,* Oxford University Press, N.Y., 1954. Dr. McNeill's work on the Celtic Penitentials and then this on Calvin do much to correct areas of Calvinism that have been incorrectly associated with the Reformer himself.

Menninger, Karl; with, Mayman, Martin, and Pruyser, Paul, *The Vital Balance: The Life Process in Mental Health and Illness,* Viking

Press, N.Y. 1963. This work by a westerner and Freudian scholar and practitioner warns against reducing diagnosis to simplistic statements and shows an awareness of balance and harmony that would please Asians.

Moltmann, Jurgen (Margaret Kohl, trans.) *Science and Wisdom,* Fortress Press, Minneapolis, 2003. A sound approach on the relation of science and religion by a sound theologian.

Murphy, Gardner, *Personality: A Biosocial Approach to Origins and Structure,* Harper and Bros., N. Y., 1947. This book should be a classic and foundational reading for any discussion of the relationship between the organic and the mental.

Nathanson, Donald L. Edit., *The Many Faces of Shame,* Guilford Press, New York, 1987.

_____,*Shame and Pride: Affect, Sex, and the Birth of the Self,* Norton, N.Y., 1992. The first of these two books brought the subject of shame into popular awareness in the field of forgiveness. The second, more profound, book, is helpful, well researched, and a seminal resource for those interested in this field.

Newell, J. Phillip, *Listening for the Heartbeat of God: A Celtic Spirituality* This clearly written book shows not only the relationship of context and instrument and the correlation of forgiveness and creativity, but also the "other side" of the Pelagian/ Augustinian controversy.

Ocker, Christopher, *Biblical Poetics Before Humanism and Reformation,* Cambridge University Press, Edinburgh, UK,2002. Another book in which one finds some of the dimensions of context and instrument as underpinnings for the days of the Reformation.

Oskamp, Stuart, and Schulz, P. W., *Applied Social Psychology,* Prentice Hall, Upper Saddle River, New Jersey, 1998. This book is an excellent source for research models and the understanding of personal and interpersonal relationships - essential to know for those in the area of pastoral theology.

Pannenberg, Wolfhart,; Bromley, Geoffrey W., translator, *Systematic Theology, Vols. I, II, & III,* Published in the U. S. by Wm. B. Eerdmans, Grand Rapids, Mi; Vol I in 1991, Vol. II in 1994, Vol. III in 1998. Volumes I and II develop the correlation of field theory and the Holy Spirit.

Parsons, Talcott, *Social Structure and Personality,* The Free Press, Macmillan, 1964. An old but good book that speaks of the community dimension of personality and forms a background for looking at the literature on the influence of environment on brain development.

Penfield, Wilder, *The Mystery of the Mind, A Critical Study of Consciousness and the Human Brain,* Princeton University Press, Princeton, NJ, 1975 This basic book by Dr. Penfield takes seriously the qualitative difference between the mind and the brain, and yet has the integrity to include a chapter by one who disagrees with the author.

Restak, Richard M., *The Mind,* Bantam Books, New York, 1988. This book is basic, well written and has excellent diagrams of the brain.

Rogers, Carl R. *Client-Centered Therapy: Its Current Practice, Implications, and Theory,* Houghton Mifflin Co., Boston, 1951. This book provides a basic view of a "client centered" process of therapy.

_____and Rosalind F. Dymond, *Psychotherapy and Personality Change,* The University of Chicago Press, 1954. Rogers and Dymond gave a basic research approach for looking at human dynamics.

Roland, Alan, *In Search of Self in India and Japan—Toward a Cross-Cultural Psychology,* Princeton University Press, Princeton, NJ, 1988. The author helps the westerner get out of the western frame of reference when looking at understandings of the mind and personality.

Rollins, Wayne G., *Soul and Psyche,* Fortress Press, Minneapolis, 1999, This book helps in dealing with the different ways in which these words have been used.

Russell, Robert J. Murphy, Nancy; Meyering, Theo C; Arbib, Michael A.; Editors, *Neuroscience and the Person: Scientific Perspectives on Divine Action,* Vatican Observatory Publications, Vatican City State and Center for Theology and the Natural Sciences, Berkeley, CA., 2002. This collection of foundational articles by leaders in the field is a basic text for examining the many facets of neuroscience and theology.

Shanks, Norman, *Iona- God's Energy: The Spirituality and Vision of the Iona Community* Hodder & Stoughton, London, 1999. This book shows the interplay between context and instrument that also correlates with the discussions in first chapters of this book on field theory and the Holy Spirit.

Siegel, Daniel J., *The Developing Mind: How Relationships and the Brain Interact to Shape Who We Are,* Guilford Press, N. Y., 1999.

This book does what the title implies and is most helpful as a beginning point in brain studies.

Smith, Archie and Riedel-Pfaefflin, *Siblings by Choice,* Chalice Press, St. Louis, 2004. This excellent book carries the matter of choice from the personal dimensions of forgiveness into the public arena of living.

Thistlethwaite, Susan Brooks, Edit., *Adam, Eve, and the Gnome— The Human Gnome Project and Theology.,* Fortress Press, Minneapolis, 2003 This book gives a fascinating discussion of myth and science.

K. H. Ting, *Love Never Ends,* Janice Wickeri, Editor and translator, Yilin Press, Nanjing 2000. This book, with its view of God as a God of Love rather than a God of punishment, gives an Asian sense of the importance of context in understanding forgiveness.

Trattner, Walter, *From Poor Law to Welfare State,* Free Press, MacMillan, NY., 1974 The author gives an evaluative history of social history approaches to poverty and concludes with an affirmation of the work of the Community Service Society, New York City.

United States Catholic Conference, *Rite of Penance,* US Catholic Conference, Washington, D. C, 1975. This report gives a post Vatican II understanding of penance and its practice.

Varela, Francisco J.; Thomson, Evan; Rosch, Eleanor; *The Embodied Mind: Cognitive Science and Human Experience,* MIT Press, Cambridge, 1993. This book is a good example of describing incarnation in cognitive rather than theological terms.

Whitehead, Alfred North, *Process and Reality,* Harper Torchbook, Harper Bros.; Macmillan, 1929. Process Philosophy shows how one can think creatively not just about philosophy but about any area of thought that deals with field theory and the process dimensions of any science.

Worthington, Everett, L., Edit., *Dimensions of Forgiveness: Psychological and Theological Perspectives,* Templeton Foundation Press, Philadelphia, 1998. Dr. Worthington has a foundational grasp of the correlation between psychology and theology.

Zhang Longxi, *The Tao and the Logos: Literary Hermeneutics, East and West,* Duke University Press., Durham, 1992. This book is one of the most profound studies I have seen of the correlation between the Asian word "Tao," and the Greek or western word, "Logos."

# Acknowledgements

In addition to those mentioned in the dedication and in the opening pages of this book, I must not close without acknowledging several groups of people to whom I am deeply indebted.

To begin with, I am grateful to the people of the Lloyd Pastoral Counseling Center at San Francisco Theological Seminary. The Rev. Dr. Sandra Brown, former director, persisted in reminding me of the need for an update of my earlier work on forgiveness. Dr. Scott Sullender, the current director, gave me opportunity to discuss some of these thoughts with graduate students at the Center.

Especially, I express appreciation to Steven and Kelli Burrill who introduced Margaret and me to key researchers at the University of California Medical Center research division. There, Dr. Cynthia Kenyon and Dr. Alan Basbaum introduced me to Catherine Bushnell who put me in touch with Tom Farrow. Without that series of contacts, this book could never have been written.

The Graduate Theological Union in Berkeley California, President James Donahue, and Dean Arthur Holder accepted me as a Visiting Scholar, and the library provided me with space and encouragement for my research at the library.

The Rev. Elisabeth Elkhart and the people of her parish, St. Marks Lutheran Church in San Francisco, permitted me rental space at a most fair price for my actual writing. At the Sequoias Retirement Community, my breakfast companions gave me guidance and insight through the long process.

Ultimately, I thank the people of Author House for their patience and understanding with the delays of presenting the manuscript to them. With the patience of JR Harris, Matthew Monroe, Amy Stout, Janelle Gonyea and my wife, and the encouragement of all our family, I offer this effort. I pray that it may be a contribution to excellence in the ministry of care. James G. Emerson, Jr.

# A Partial List of References

## An Index

**(Footnotes)**

[1] Emerson, James G, *Divorce, the Church and Remarriage,* Westminster Press, Philadelphia 1959, Page 26.

[2] Dennett, Daniel C., *Consciousness Explained,* Little Brown and Co., Boston, 1991; p 210.

[3] Ibid. p 279.

[4] Rogers, Carl and Dymond, Rosalind, *Psychotherapy and Personality Change,* The University of Chicago, Press, Chicago, 1954, p. 13.

[5] Blakemore, Susan: *Consciousness: An Introduction,* Oxford University Press, New York, 2004 gives a marvelous discussion of Rene Descartes on page 12 and succeeding pages of her excellent book.

[6] Arbib, M. A. as in N*euroscience and the Person: Scientific Perspectives on Divine Action,* The Vatican Observatory Publications, the Vatican City State, and The Center for Theology and the Natural Sciences, Berkeley, CA. 2002, p 81.

[7] Ibid.

[8] Koch, Christof, *The Quest for Consciousness: A Neurobiological Approach,* Roberts and Company Publishers, Englewood, Colorado, 2004, p. 327.

[9] Ibid.

[10] It is this phenomenon that gives a basis for the philosophical writings of men like Berkeley and religious views such those expressed in the Christian Science book *Science and Health with Key to the Scriptures.*

[11] For much of this section, I am indebted not only to Christof Koch but also to the writing of Susan Blakemore's book *Consciousness: An Introduction,* Oxford University Press, New York, 2004 and Richard Restak's *The Mind,* Bantam Books, Toronto, 1988; the work of Kelly Bulkeley , Mark Graves, at the GTU. The application of the concept of a field, however, is mine.

[12] Restak, Richard M., *The Mind,* Bantam Books, New York, 1988 p. 26. Although the material above is common to many books on the brain and the mind, Dr. Restak's pictures are the most helpful.

[13] Ibid. Lewin, p. xi.

[14] Ibid. p. ix.

[15] Eg. an article in *Science, Vo. 300, April 4, 2002,* pp 76-77 by Scott Fraser (California Institute of Technology ) Stephan Smith (Stanford) and Jeff Lichtman, (Washington U. St Louis)

[16] Again, I call attention to Susan Blakemore's presentation on the various views and arguments about the idea of a "self" or a "mind" or "consciousness." Above, I have stated simply where I come out in that discussion as a basis for getting on to the experience of forgiveness itself.

[17] Allport, Gordon, *Becoming,* New Haven: Yale University Press, 1955

[18] Ibid. page 40

[19] Ibid . 67

[20] Daniel J. Siegel, *The Developing Mind, How Relationships and the Brain Interact to Shape Who We Are,* The Guilford Press, New York, 1999, pp. 70-120

[21] In private papers made available to me by her husband shortly after her death

[22] Nathanson, Donald L., *Shame and Pride: Affect, Sex, and the Birth of the Self,* 1992, pp145-6.

[23] Cooper-White, Pamela, *The Cry of Tamar; Violence Against Women and the Church's Response,* Fortress Press, Minneapolis, 1995, pp. 4 ff.

[24] Ibid Nathanson , pp. 19 and 15

[25] Daniel J. Siegel, *The Developing Mind: How Relationships and the Brain Interact to Shape Who We Are*
Guildford Press, NY, 1999, p. 24.

[26] Ibid. , Restak, pg 257 – also Arbib, *Science and the Person,* 2002, p 88, 97.

[27] Gardner Murphy, *Personality: A Biosocial Approach to Origins and Structure,* Harper and Bros., , 1947, p. 991.

[28] Ibid. pp. 366-7

[29] *Science,* Vol. 300, June 13, 2003, page 1755.

[30] *Science,* Vol 270, 1995 pp. 769-775

[31] Feldman, *From Molecule to Metaphor, MIT press,* p. 16

[32] This source is all from *The Theological Dictionary of the Old Testament Vol. IV,* G. Johannes Botterweck and Helmer Ringgren, editors, and David E. Green, translator, Erdman Publishing, Grand Rapids, Michigan, 1980, pp65 ff.

[33] *Theological Dictionary of the New Testament, Vol IV,* Gerhard Kittel, Editor. Geoffrey W. Bromley, Translator, Eerdmans Publishing Co, Grand Rapids, MI., 1967, pp 675 and following.

[34] *Science March 23 page, 1479*

[35] Ibid, Seigel

[36] Francis Crick as in *Nature, Vo. 337, January 12, 1989, page 129.*

[37] Ibid. p 132

[38] J. Feldman, Ibid., p 3

[39] Hakwsan C. Lau, e al, *Science,* Vo. 303, February 20, 2004 , pp 1208 ff.

[40] *Science,* Vo. 303 January 9, 2004, p. 233.

[41] *Science,* Vol 304, May 7, 2004, p. 828

[42] Siegel , Ibid. Note particularly sections on attachment and integration.

[43] Siegel, Ibid.

[44] Erika L. Sanborne, MA, of Andover Newton Theological School, Newton MA.I

[45] *Science*, Vol. 3, February 20, 2004 p. 1157

[46] Luiz Pessos, *Science,* "Seeing the World in the Same Way," Vol 303, March 12, 2004 p. 1617

[47] Ibid

[48] Ibid, Koch, p.100

[49] It is at this point that I have concern about many of the recent studies on the brain. Too often, those studies act as though nothing has happened between the days of Sigmund Freud, William James, and Isaac Newton on the one hand, and the days of the MRI and all that such tools have opened up to us. In his writings on the matter of perspective,[50] Professor Feldman brings together the understandings of interpersonal dynamics over the past one hundred years ago and today.

[51] Emerson, James, *The Dynamics of Forgiveness,* Westminster Pres, Philadelphia, 1964, p.43.

[52] *Holy Qur'an,* trans. M. H. Shakir, Tahrike Tarsile Qur'an, Inc., Elmhurst, N.Y. Third Edition 1985, p.

[53] Gerhard von Rad, *Genesis: A Commentary,* Revised Edition, Westminster Press, 1961, p. 46

[54] Ibid. Pannenberg, pp 382-3

[55] Lao Tze, *Tao The Ching,* John C. H. Wu trans., Shambhala, Boston and London, 1989 p.

[56] Ibid, Nathan, p 17.

[57] William Gesenius, *Hebrew and Chaldee Lexicon,* tr. By S. P. Tregells, Wm. B. Eerdmans Publishing Co., 1949. p 588

[58] Robert B. Girdlestone, *Synonyms of the Old Testament,* William B Eerdmans Publishing Company [a reprint of 1897], 1948, p.135

[59]

[60] *The Rite of Penance, Study Edition,* United States Catholic Conference, Publication Office, Washington D.C, 1975

[61] Farrow in a private letter to me.

[62] Smith, Archie and Riedel, Ursula, *Siblings by Choice: Race, Gender, and Violence, 2994, Chalice Press, St. Louis Mo.*

[63] Ibid page 4

[64] Mckee, *Katharina Schütz Zell,*Vol I, Brill, Boston, 1999 – page 470 ff

# About the Author

**James G. Emerson, Jr.,** better known as Jim, is a visiting scholar at the Graduate Theological Union in Berkeley, California; an adjunct professor at San Francisco Theological Seminary; and pastor emeritus of Calvary Presbyterian Church. He is author of *Divorce, the Church, and Remarriage, The Dynamics of Forgiveness,* and *Suffering: Its Meaning and Ministry* (1987 choice for the "Book of the Year" award of the Academy of Pastoral Clergy.) He serves on the editorial boards of *Pastoral Psychology* and *The Journal of Pastoral Care.* Jim served as General Director of the Community Service Society of New York City during its major study of that city in the 1970s. Jim also served two years as Interim President of San Francisco Theological Seminary at the turn of this century.

He and his wife are trained as counselors. For the past six years, Jim has concentrated on studies of the brain and the role of the brain in the experience of forgiveness.